THE NE JOY OF DISCOVERY IN BIBLE STUDY

NEWLY REVISED

Oletta Wald

Augsburg Fortress
Minneapolis

THE NEW JOY OF DISCOVERY IN BIBLE STUDY

Cover: Alan Furst

ISBN 978-0-8066-4429-5

Manufactured in the U.S.A.

12 11 10 09 9 10 11 12

Contents

Introduction

This book is a new, revised edition of the book *The Joy of Discovery in Bible Study*. Oletta Wald wrote the first edition soon after attending the former Biblical Seminary in New York, where she was introduced to *inductive Bible study*. This book calls the process *discovery Bible study*. While this new edition contains the same basic principles described in the first and the revised editions, the format has been changed and the material rearranged, using inclusive language and the New Revised Version Bible (NRSV). The focus continues to be only on Bible *study*. The section on Bible *teaching* is included in a companion book: *The New Joy of Teaching Discovery Bible Study*. The purpose of this book is to engage readers in learning Bible study skills that will encourage them to become discoverers in Bible study, and experience joy in the process. The following is the introduction written by Oletta Wald for the revised edition of *The Joy of Discovery in Bible Study* published in 1975:

A "Flounderer" in Bible Study

I had been a student of the Bible several years before I become a discoverer on my own. I could follow the suggestions of others and answer the questions they asked, but I floundered when I tried to launch out on my own. I did not know where to start or what to do. The treasures of the Bible seemed locked behind abstract words. I always had to depend on someone else to open the door.

Learning the Secret

While a student at the former Biblical Seminary in New York, I was taught how to explore the truths of the Bible in a methodical and systematic way. I learned some steps to take when studying a passage. I found that it was like working a combination lock. When I followed the steps, the Word opened up to me. I felt free. I realized that I was no longer dependent on others to gain insights into Scripture. I had become a discoverer. In a new way, Bible study became more meaningful and personal. Most of all it was deeply satisfying to know how to discover the truths in God's Word. I had experienced the joy of discovery in Bible study!

Sharing My Discoveries with Others

My new discoveries were too good to keep to myself. I began to teach the skills to my students at the Lutheran Bible Institute and to lay people in congregations. I found that whenever people would conscientiously apply the principles and follow the steps, they too became discoverers and experienced greater joy in their Bible study. Therefore I wrote *The Joy of Discovery in Bible Study*. Initially I wrote the book for students in colleges and seminaries.

Need for Revision

Since the writing of the first edition of *The Joy of Discovery*, I realized the necessity of revising the book to better meet these needs of those who were using it in congregations:

Need to introduce the skills gradually: If learners are introduced to too many skills at one time or spend too little time on each skill, they can become frustrated and discouraged. They may think that the process is too difficult and reject the validity of the skills.

Need for satisfaction: When learning a skill, there is always some frustration. In the process, learners have to experience enough satisfaction to want to continue learning.

Need for recognizing varied abilities: Responses to these discovery skills will vary according to learners' interests and background, but all can find a measure of satisfaction in the process.

Pattern for the Revisions

I introduce the skills from the easy to the more complex. The book is divided into two phases: Part One: The Discovering Phase, chapters 1 to 6; and Part Two: The Expanding Phase, chapters 7 to 14. If you are interested in learning the basics of discovery Bible study, you might find Part One enough. If you are interested in learning how to go deeper into Bible study, you will want to continue in Part Two. The skills will be introduced gradually enough for you to grasp the process, and also be challenging enough to motivate your study.

My Indebtedness

The methods presented in this book are not new. They have been advocated by biblical scholars through the years. One of the greatest exponents of methodical Bible study was the late Dr. Wilbur W. White, founder of the Biblical Seminary in New York, now called the New York Seminary. The principles Dr. White set forth have been proclaimed by his successors at the seminary and by its countless graduates in all parts of the world. These principles are the background for this book.

I am indebted to many fine teachers at the Biblical Seminary who taught me the methodical principles of Bible study, but in a special way to Professor Robert Traina, whose book *Methodical Bible Study* is the basis for this manual. I am grateful to Mr. Traina for permission to use his book as a basis.

My Hope

The purpose of this book is to help you become a discoverer in Bible study and experience joy in the process. Most of the chapters contain information about the discovery skills and practice that will help you develop the skills. You will learn very little unless you practice the suggested skills. They are the most important aspects of the book. Since the purpose of this resource is to teach you *how* to study, do not be too concerned about how right or wrong you are in what you are doing. As you practice some of the skills, you will realize that you are learning to *discover* some of the truths in a passage. Do not become discouraged in the process. Learning skills does take time. The Lord will increase your capacity to gain deeper insight into the Word as you pray, practice, and persevere. Give the Word—and yourself—time!

1 The Joy of Discovery

Bible study can be fun! Maybe that statement startles you. Possibly you have always thought that Bible study should be somber and serious. Maybe you are thinking, "Isn't this the book inspired by God's Spirit? Shouldn't Bible study be approached in a spirit of humility and seriousness? *Fun* is *merriment, playful action*, a *game*. Does this mean that Bible study should be treated like a playful game?"

Fun in this context does not mean any of these things. This statement is not speaking about the purpose of Bible study, but the process. It is possible to find the process in Bible study engaging, challenging, and a joy. It is possible to have been involved in a study and afterward say, "Wow, we had a good time today in our study!" This is the kind of fun meant—a joyful experience because you were learning how to become a discoverer of God's Word and found the process a joy!

The Joy of Discovery—a Possibility for All

One of the goals of this book is to enable you to become a discoverer and experience the joy that can be yours in the process. While all Christians agree that the Bible should be studied, some do not find joy in their study. Others have been students of the Bible for many years and already know the joy there is in the study. Maybe some of you are still in high school. Many of you are adult learners. Some of you are leaders, teachers, or missionaries who are guiding others in Bible studies.

How can one book challenge such a variety of people in terms of age, experience, and background? It couldn't if it were not that you all have one thing in common. You are using this book because you have a deep yearning to learn more about how to study the Bible. The hope and prayer of the author is that you can begin where you are and, through the suggestions in this book, develop your potentials as *discoverers*.

Why Become Discoverers?

According to the dictionary, to *discover* is to obtain insight or knowledge the first time, to ascertain, unearth, explore. A discoverer is one who finds out something for herself or himself.

The pattern in many Bible study groups is for the leader to be the *discoverer* and share the discoveries with others. Since the participants are not helped to become discoverers, they can quickly forget what was taught. Through the suggestions in this resource, you will learn how to become your own discoverer and to remember what you discover in God's Word.

It is possible to learn the skills in discovery Bible study and gain only intellectual knowledge, but this need not happen, nor is it likely. The pianist or the star baseball player masters the skills of playing so that mechanics become second nature and she or he is able to play at her or his best. In the same way, when you learn some of these skills, you will gain deeper insights into the truths in the Bible and the Holy Spirit will have a freer course in your life.

Practice, patience, and perseverance are needed for learning any skill. As you practice the skills described in this book, gradually you will experience:

- the joy of discovering truths in the Bible yourself.
- the joy of realizing that the Bible has something special to say to you personally.
- the joy of discovering your own potential as a student.
- the joy of sharing with others the truths that have special meaning to you.
- the joy of knowing that the Holy Spirit is the revealer of truth as you seek to discover the Word.
- the joy of discovering Jesus Christ as the incarnate Word.

Discovering with Others

You can become a discoverer in Bible study by yourself. It is possible to follow the suggestions in this resource and learn some of the keys to Bible study. But you can multiply the effectiveness of your study by working together in a small group. If you are using this book with a group in a congregation or school situation, you already are involved with others in the study. If not, consider inviting three or four others to study with you.

In discovery Bible study there is value in team learning. While you may have a leader to be your guide, your most significant learning can be from the participants in your small group, your team members. Even though you may be in a large class, try to work in teams of about four people:

1. Each of you works individually on the suggested practice exercises in each section titled "Discovery Skills."

2. Come together and share your insights, enlarging your understanding as you share.

3. Sometimes you may divide the tasks and each concentrate on only one segment of the passage. In this way, you can accomplish a more thorough study and gain greater insights.

4. The role of the leader is to be your enabler—the one who enables the members of the group to becomes discoverers and sharers.

To summarize, there is value in learning as part of a small group. Team learning:

Develops self-responsibility: Team learning helps you exercise self-responsibility for your own learning. But it also calls for shared responsibility on the part of your teammates. You cannot expect to learn from one another until you first do some discovering by yourselves.

Increases satisfaction and learning: Two heads are better than one. As you study a segment, you will find that each team member discovers different things. Your satisfaction will be derived first through your own discoveries and secondly through those received from others. No one can discover all of the riches of God's Word by herself or himself.

Develops your creative potential: By practicing some of the skills described in this resource, you will find you can discover some of the truths in Scripture and that others are enriched by your discoveries. Effective team learning depends on the willingness of all members to share, listen, challenge, and question each other. Through this process you will learn to clarify your own thinking, refine your insights, broaden your concepts, and correct faulty ones.

NOTE: Read Chapter 14, Discovering with Others, for more detailed discussion on the value of studying with others.

2

How to Become a Discoverer

As you begin discovery Bible study, first consider the attitudes that will hinder or help you.

Attitudes that Hinder

The defeated: I won't be able to understand anything anyway, so why try to study the Bible?

The negative: I would like to learn how to study the Bible better, but I doubt that anything I discover would be any good. I am afraid to express any ideas because I fear they may be wrong.

The closed heart: I don't believe everything the Bible teaches. Since it was written so many hundreds of years ago, how can it have any value today? So why study it?

The lazy: I suppose if I tried I could understand more than I do, but what I read seems rather hard and dull. I don't know if I want to invest the energy to learn how to study.

Attitudes that Help

The positive: I want to learn how to study the Bible. No doubt I will have trouble learning some of the Bible study skills. I am sure there will be things in the Bible I will not understand. But I believe that through the help of the Holy Spirit I can learn how to gain insight into God's Word.

The reflective: God asks of me only an open heart and an open mind so I can access God's truths and revelation. I don't have to understand everything.

The expectant: I am coming to the Word to let God speak to me. It is good to know that I don't have to try to squeeze truths out of it. As I study and pray, I believe that the message in any scripture passage will unfold itself to me.

The faithful: I cannot expect much from Bible study unless I am willing to invest some energy and discipline in the study. I need faithfulness and diligence. If I only scratch the surface, my reward will be a few crumbs. If I dig deeply into the Word, my reward will be rich treasures.

Approaches to Bible Study

Usually you study the Bible with some definite purpose in mind. Possibly you have been invited to conduct a Bible study at a meeting or you are to teach a church school class. Or you may be studying it on your own for personal inspiration. Whatever your reason, there are several approaches you can use.

Hit-and-miss approach: You might read a passage several times. You may write down some of the ideas you gain in the reading. You might read another translation or a commentary. You may spend some time thinking and praying about what you read. In all of this, you do not follow a logical pattern.

The application approach: This is one of the most common approaches. You quickly read the passage and then spend your time thinking about ways it might be applied to life.

The commentary approach: You read the Bible passage and then immediately read some commentaries for further insight. You let the commentary be your teacher.

The Holy Spirit approach: You spend most of your study time in prayer and meditation. You read the passage and then look to the Holy Spirit to reveal to you the insights and truths in the passage without doing any serious study.

The methodical approach: In this type you follow an orderly and logical pattern to study the Bible. This approach does not discount the validity of the other approaches but incorporates them when appropriate. If you hope to become a discoverer, challenge yourself to develop an orderly and logical procedure in your study. In doing so you will find that you gain more insight and greater satisfaction.

Process in Methodical Bible Study

Method implies a regular order. If you desire to develop a methodical pattern in your study of the Bible, there are definite procedures to follow, and it is best if they are done in a certain order. On page 13 is a list of some of the steps in discovery Bible study and their most logical order. These procedures can be true in all study, not just Bible study. As you read the list, think about how you follow these procedures even when you are reading the daily newspaper.

Why This Emphasis on Logical Steps?

There is real value in deliberately trying to do one step at the time. Most people accomplish the most when concentrating on one thing at a time. This is especially true when first trying to understand something, whether it is a piece of literature, a scientific problem, or a Bible passage.

Scientists make no interpretation and draw no conclusion until they have observed thoroughly all the facts. So it should be with you as a Bible student. First *observe!* No interpreting, no applying—until you have observed carefully *all* that is written!

This emphasis on the logical approach does not discount the importance of the Holy Spirit as the revealer of truth. The Holy Spirit will guide you as you observe, interpret, evaluate, apply, and actualize. It is precisely the Spirit's involvement in the process that enables you to be alert in your observations, discerning in your interpretations, honest in your evaluations and applications, and courageous in actualizing the truths in your own life.

Steps in Discovery Bible Study

1. OBSERVE exactly what the author has written.	This is the most important step in Bible study and must come first. The more careful and thorough your observations, the more meaningful will be your interpretations, the fairer will be your evaluations, and the richer will be your applications.
2. INTERPRET objectively what the author has written.	After you have observed carefully what the author has written, determine what it means. Try to discover the thoughts, attitudes, emotions, and purpose of the author.
3. SUMMARIZE concisely the key ideas in a passage.	While summarization is listed as step 3, it really is a process that should be done in connection with both observation and interpretation. Summarize the facts that you observe and the meaning of the facts.
4. EVALUATE fairly what the author has written.	Not until you have a clear concept of what the author writes and means can you honestly judge the importance of the passage. Thus evaluation must come after observation and interpretation.
5. APPLY personally the message revealed.	Application is the fruit that comes forth through the other steps. Application is a growing process, not superimposed in a superficial way, but rising out of all the other steps.
6. ACTUALIZE your convictions.	Someone has said, "Don't just study the Bible, *do* something!"

Tools for Bible Study

A basic study Bible: Use an accepted standard version for your basic study Bible. If your Bible is old and has small print, buy a new one. There are many basic versions to select from such as the *New King James Version, New Revised Standard Version, New English Bible, New American Standard,* or *The New International Version.* All of these are based on original manuscripts. The translators have tried to be as accurate as possible in translating from the early manuscripts. All of the illustrations used in this resource are taken from the *New Revised Standard Version.*

Several translations and paraphrases: Besides one basic study Bible, you should have several other translations. Among these you might want to have some of the more "free" translations and paraphrases, such as *The Living Bible, Today's English Version (Good News Bible), Contemporary English Version (CEV), New Living Translation, Phillips,* or *Amplified Version.* All of these will give you insight into the meaning of words.

Concordance: A concordance is an alphabetical index to help you find Bible passages on particular subjects. You may have one in the back of one of your Bibles. A concordance is useful for finding cross-references.

Dictionary: A dictionary is a very important tool in Bible study. Looking up definitions of key words will give you new insight into meanings.

Commentaries, Bible dictionary, Bible atlas: These are very helpful in providing background to the geography, history, and culture of biblical times, as well as insight into some of the difficult passages.

Electronic Bible study resources: All the types of resources named here are available in electronic versions. Some are on CD-ROM and may be purchased from Christian bookstores or the catalogs of Christian publishers. Others are available to download from the Internet. Try a search for "Bible study resources" to discover the rich variety of materials available online.

3

Begin by Learning to See!

The first skill to develop is to train your mind to *see* when you read a passage—to observe carefully the words, to be on the alert for the details. Inaccurate and careless observations can lead to faulty interpretations and shallow applications.

Meaning and Purpose of Observation

Observation can be defined in several ways: the act, power, or habit of seeing and noting; to watch closely; to look intently; to give full attention to what one sees; to be mentally aware of what one sees. Someone described observation as "the art of seeing things as they are, impartially, intensely, fearlessly."

The purpose of observation is to saturate yourself thoroughly with the content of a passage. Like a sponge, absorb everything before you. Learn to be exact and accurate in your observations. Not everything you read will be of equal value; therefore, in the process you also have to learn to discern what is noteworthy and what is not. All of these procedures require concentration.

Ways to Observe

To "see" more when you read, you may find that you need "handles" or clues, help in knowing what specific things to observe. Once you learn some of the specific things to look for, you will begin to discover things in your reading that you never saw before.

Learning to observe details is a skill that will take time and practice. On the next two pages are charts containing a list of the kinds of things to look for when reading a passage. This list is a quick overview. In the following chapters, the items on the list will be described in greater detail.

The list includes many components so you can become familiar with the variety of things to look for in Bible study, but learning to observe is like any other skill. You will learn it a step at a time.

Learning the skills in observation requires concentrated thinking. Keep this in mind if you become frustrated in learning how to develop your powers of observation.

Practice Skills

To learn the skills of observation takes practice. While the list includes many skills, you will practice only a few at a time. Gradually as you practice, observing details will become second nature to you. On pages 19-23 are some Discovery Skills to practice. Don't just read the suggestions. Actually do them, one practice skill at a time. Your powers of observation will increase as you follow the suggestions.

Specific Things to Observe

Key Words	When you first read a passage, look for the key words; those words you think are important in the passage. Repetition of words will sometimes give you a clue. Underline them in your Bible.
Advice **Admonitions** **Warnings** **Promises**	Be on the alert for the admonitions a writer gives: the advice, the exhortations, the warnings, and the things the text tells you to do. Also note the promises and the encouragements. One clue is to look for imperative verbs.
Reasons **Results**	When you observe admonitions, see if the writer gives you some reasons for any advice. Or note if there is a cause-and-effect relationship—*if* you do this, *then* this will happen. Often with a warning, the writer will give possible results.
Contrast **Comparisons** **Illustrations**	Make special note of the way a writer uses contrasts, comparisons, and illustrations to bring out the ideas. Comparisons and contrasts point out similarities and differences.
Repetition and Progression of Ideas	Be alert for repetition of words, ideas, or statements. This often will give you a clue as to the author's purpose in a passage. Take special note of lists of items or ideas. Compare the items and see if there is any significance in the order. Is there a progression of ideas toward a climax?
Questions	Be on the watch for the use of the question. Is it used to introduce an idea, summarize a series of ideas, or just to challenge your thinking?

Specific Things to Observe

Important Connectives prepositions conjunctions	Connectives are very important in revealing key ideas and relationships. Be on the alert for some of the following: *but*—introduces a contrast *if*—introduces conditional clause *for, because, therefore*—introduce reason and results *in, into, with*—important connectives *in order that*—sets forth a purpose
Grammatical Construction verbs nouns pronouns adverbs adjectives	Note the grammatical construction of some statements. Be on the alert for the verbs and their tenses, for the use of pronouns, and for the use of adverbs and adjectives and the way they describe things.
Atmosphere **Emphatic Statements**	Note the general tone of a passage. It may be characterized by the mood of joy, thanksgiving, concern, humility, zeal, anger, or caution. The tone of a passage may vary as a writer moves from one idea to another. The way a writer addresses readers often reveals the mood. Also note the use of emphatic statements, words, and phrases to reveal feelings.
Literary Form	Always note the literary form of a passage: discourse, narrative, poetry, drama, parable, or apocalyptic. Also determine if the writer is using literal or figurative terms.
General Structure	Note the arrangement of the ideas in a passage, the relationship of verses to each other. Sometimes the author makes a general statement, then explains it with examples. Other times the text may list a series of ideas and then summarize with a general statement.

DISCOVERY SKILLS 1 Bible Focus: Matthew 6:25-34

Practice A—Be on Alert for Details

1. Look for key words.

The first step is always to be alert for the key words; those words that seem important to the message. This is one of the easier processes in observation, and also one of the most important. Begin by observing the words and deciding what seems to be the most important for understanding the main thrust of the passage.

On page 20 is a "structural diagram" of Matthew 6:25-34. Use this passage for your first practice. Note the way the units of thought are arranged. As you study this passage, make your observations directly on the printed passage.

a) **Underline the key words.** As you read Matthew 6:25-34, use a colored pencil to underline key words. One of the clues is to note the words that are repeated. Underline anything you think is important. There is no right or wrong—underline as much as you feel like underlining.

b) **Select the most important words.** In the process you may have underlined many words, or just a few. If you have underlined many, your next task is to determine which of the many are *the* key words. Not all of the underlined words may have equal value. Review what you have underlined and select those you think are most significant in terms of the message in the passage. Circle these words.

2. Look for other details.

Looking for key words gives you some insight into the passage, but this is just a beginning. To gain more insight, record in the left margin of the passage other observations:

- admonitions and reasons
- use of questions
- contrasts, comparisons, illustrations
- key connectives *(circle these)*
- repetition of ideas
- emphatic statements

Matthew 6:25-34

25. "Therefore I tell you,
 do not worry about your life,
 what you will eat or
 what you will drink,
 or about your body,
 what you will wear.
 Is not life more than food,
 and the body more than clothing?
26. Look at the birds of the air;
 they neither sow nor reap
 nor gather into barns,
 and yet your heavenly Father feeds them.
 Are you not of more value than they?
27. And can any of you by worrying
 add a single hour to your span of life?
28. And why do you worry about clothing?
 Consider the lilies of the field,
 how they grow;
 they neither toil nor spin,
29. yet I tell you,
 even Solomon in all his glory
 was not clothed like one of these.
30. But if God so clothes the grass of the field,
 which is alive today
 and tomorrow is thrown into the oven,
 will he not much more clothe you,
 —you of little faith?
31. Therefore do not worry, saying,
 'What will we eat?'
 or 'What will we drink?'
 or 'What will we wear?'
32. For it is the Gentiles who strive for all these things;
 and indeed your heavenly Father knows
 that you need all these things.
33. But strive first for the kingdom of God and his righteousness,
 and all these things
 will be given to you as well.
34. "So do not worry about tomorrow,
 for tomorrow will bring worries of its own.
 Today's trouble is enough for today.

Example

Observations	**Scripture Passage**
Important connective: *therefore*	25. "Therefore
Emphatic statement: *I tell you*	I tell you,
Admonition: *do not worry*	do not worry about
Key words: *worry, life*	your life,
Two illustrations: *eat,*	what you will eat
drink	or what you will drink,
Other things not to worry about:	or about your body,
body, what you will wear	what you will wear.
Note use of question.	Is not life more than food,
Note repetition of words: *life, body,*	and the body more than
more	clothing?

This is an example of how you might record observations on the printed Bible passage, or you might record the observation and draw a line to the word or group of words about which you are making the observation.

3. Look for general structure.

Remember that one of the things to observe is the general structure of a passage: the relationship of the verses to each other. Always bracket verses that seem to focus on the same topic. One way to bracket these verses may be: 6:25; 26-27; 28-30; 31-34. Then summarize the main idea in each set of verses in brief phrases.

This passage is an example of progression on ideas. Determine which verse is the climax of the passage.

Practice B—Seek to Know Meanings

1. Begin by asking yourself questions.

Possibly you have asked yourself, "I wonder why Jesus said the things he did? I wonder what he meant by what he said?" Asking yourself questions is an important step in Bible study. It is the bridge between observation and interpretation. These questions might be called *I wonder* questions or *questions for understanding.*

Learning to ask ourselves questions about what we read is a skill just like learning how to observe. At first many people may not know how to ask themselves questions. In Chapter 6 there is more detail on the process of asking questions, but here are some questions you can ask yourself now:

- Why did Jesus say . . . ?
- What is the meaning of . . . ?

- What is the significance of . . . ?
- What is the implication of . . . ?
- What is the relationship between . . . ?

Example

Scripture Passage	Questions for Understanding
25. "Therefore	Why the emphatic words,
I tell you,	*I tell you?*
do not worry about	Meaning of *worry?*
your life,	Meaning of *life?*
what you will eat	Significance of these illustrations?
or what you will drink,	
or about your body,	Meaning of *body?*
what you will wear.	Significance of this illustration?
Is not life more than food,	Significance of this question?
and the body more than	Symbolic meaning of *food* and
clothing?	*clothing?*

These are just examples of the kinds of questions you might ask yourself. Write down some of the questions you have.

2. Answer questions.

Asking questions stimulates your thinking and helps you identify those words, phrases, and statements that need interpretation. Maybe you thought that words such as *worry, body,* and *life* did not need interpretation. But when you begin to ask yourself questions about them, you realize that you need to interpret them in order to fully understand the passage.

Chapter 6 discusses more thoroughly the ways to interpret a passage; this chapter suggests only a few ways. Try to answer some of your questions by doing these things:

a) Define words: Look in a dictionary to discover the meaning of some of the key words such as *worry, life, body, kingdom, righteousness.*

b) Compare translations: Read the passage in several translations to discover what other words are used in translating the passage.

c) Study cross-references: Luke 12:22-31; Romans 14:17; Philippians 4:4-7.

d) Wrestle with meanings: It is possible to define words, compare translations, study cross-references, and still not really get at the core meaning of a passage. You also have to wrestle, think, meditate, and integrate what you have been learning, and draw conclusions.

e) **Summarize findings:** Formulate the insights gained through your study in some summary statements; for example, Jesus seems to be saying these things . . .

Practice C—Personalize Biblical Teachings

All people worry about life's necessities. In this passage Jesus seems to focus on the things that are given priority in daily life.

Evaluation

As you study this passage, ask yourself if what Jesus says has value for today. Will Jesus really supply all your needs?

Application and Actualization

Select one of the following and consider how you might apply the challenge in this passage to your life:

1. **Complete this statement:** If I really took Jesus' teaching in this passage seriously, the difference it would make in my life is . . .

2. **Analyze your worries.** Divide a sheet of paper in three parts:

List some things you are worried about right now	List some of the ways you usually handle those worries	Following Jesus' admonitions, list some ways that would be better approaches

3. **Study advertisements in magazines and newspapers.** What do they say about priorities and worries?

4. **Share and pray.** Share with others something that worries you and invite them to pray with you about it. Pray with them about their worries.

4
How to Increase Your Powers of Observation

You have just practiced the main procedures involved in any Bible study—steps to follow to discover the content and meaning of a passage. As you studied Matthew 6:25-34, you did these things:

Observed: by looking for key words, admonitions, questions, contrasts, comparisons, illustrations, connectives, and so forth.

Interpreted: by asking questions, comparing translations, defining words, studying cross-references, and wrestling with meanings.

Summarized: by bracketing verses and summarizing key ideas.

Evaluated: by determining what value Jesus' words have for people today.

Applied: by thinking of what these words were saying to you personally.

Actualized: only you know in what way you have been actualizing the admonitions in this passage.

When you tried to follow some of these steps, did you have problems? If you did, you are normal! Learning skills takes practice. But hopefully you gained a deeper insight into this passage, even though it is a passage you may have read many times—you discovered some truths you have not discovered before.

In Chapter 3 you received a list and brief descriptions of the many features to observe in a passage. To broaden your understanding of these techniques, more detailed descriptions and practice passages are included in this chapter.

1. Look for admonitions.

When you are reading a discourse passage, be on the alert for every time the writer tells you to *do something*, to *not do something*, or *to be something*. These might be admonitions, warnings, exhortations, advice, commands, or promises. The writer will be speaking directly to you, the reader. Or in the case of Jesus' admonitions, he will be speaking directly to his listeners. When you look for admonitions, note the imperative verbs, those that tell you to do something. These are often your key.

2. Look for logical relationships.

Whenever you find *commands, advice* or *warnings*, the writer will often back them up with *reasons, purposes, proofs*, or *results*. Also be on the alert for *cause-and-effect* relationships. Sometimes the writer will set forth a warning and then show the effects if the warning is not heeded. The writer may add a condition and then give the reason for the condition. Connectives are often the key for noting logical relationships. Train yourself to observe these key connectives:

- *because* or *for:* These words often introduce a reason or result.
- *in order that:* This phrase often sets forth a purpose.
- *therefore:* This word often introduces a summary of ideas, a result, or condition.
- *if:* This conjunction introduces a condition that requires action or sets forth a cause which will bring forth certain results. "*If* this is true, *then* this will happen or this should happen."

3. Look for contrasts, comparisons, illustrations.

When a passage conveys a new idea, it often will be associated with something that is already familiar to the reader. Make special note of the way the writer uses contrasts, comparisons, and illustrations. Two kinds of comparisons in grammar are similes and metaphors. An example of a simile is: "The tongue is *like* a fire." An example of a metaphor is: "The tongue *is* a fire."

A contrast points out differences. It is believed that the mind can recall contrasts better than comparisons. The connective "but" often introduces a contrast.

4. Look for repetitions and progressions in thought.

To impress the readers and communicate ideas, an author will often repeat words, phrases, or ideas. Also make special note of lists of items. Authors have reasons for listing what they do and even for the order of a series. Study the series to see if there is any significance in the order of the list or progression in thought. Compare the first and the last items in a series to see if there is any significant difference.

There can be progression in thought patterns as well as in a series of items. One idea can grow out of another. Note if the author arranges the ideas progressing toward a climax. Does one idea build on another until the greatest challenge appears at the end of a paragraph or chapter?

5. Look for grammatical constructions.

It is important to make note of some grammatical constructions. Remember that some Christian doctrines have been determined by verb tenses, singular nouns, and little prepositions such as *in* and *through!*

You do not have to identify every word in a passage in terms of its grammatical construction. This list reflects some areas for which to be alert:

- **Nouns and pronouns:** Especially be mindful of the personal pronouns.
- **Verbs and their tenses:** Often key to understanding a passage.
- **Adjectives and adverbs:** Note what they describe.
- **Key prepositions:** Note the significance of such words as *in, through, into, by, of.*
- **Important connectives:** Be mindful of the connectives that reflect results, reasons, and conclusions, such as *therefore, yet, however, likewise, nevertheless.*
- **Emphatic words:** Note words and phrases that the author uses to give emphasis such as *truly, verily, behold, indeed, finally, especially, last of all, I tell you.*
- **Phrases and clauses:** Note what they describe. Note how some clauses are introduced with the words *who, where, when, what, why, how*. These are also words you might use as questions when you are observing a passage.

You will find that as you look for other things, you will begin to identify some of these grammatical constructions as well.

6. Look for use of questions.

A writer may use a question to introduce an idea, to challenge the thinking of the readers, or to summarize. Sometimes there are rhetorical questions that do not expect an answer, but stimulate the thinking of the reader and challenge a response.

7. Look for the general structure of the passage.

Be mindful of the structure of a biblical passage, whether it is a paragraph, a chapter, or even a book. Structure can often reveal an author's purpose. You will find clues in the words and in the arrangement of the ideas. Sometimes they may be in a logical order, one idea growing out of the next; this reveals concern for intellectual impact. Other times the ideas appear in a psychological order, revealing concern for the emotional impact. Sometimes, Bible passages seem to have no apparent order in terms of structure. The ideas are more like beads on a string, or they tumble out in profusion like Paul's ideas in some of his epistles.

Be alert for the relationship between verses and paragraphs. Make note of those verses that seem to focus on the same ideas. Also note whether a writer begins with a general statement and continues with specific examples, or starts with a series of ideas and summarizes with a general statement.

8. Look for literary form and atmosphere.

Literary form is the type of writing an author uses to express a message. As you study a passage, observe the following types:

- **Discourse:** the kind of approach found in Jesus' sermons and employed in the epistles, in which ideas are presented in logical and argumentative form.
- **Prose narrative:** found in the historical books and the Gospels, where historical events are often described in chronological order.
- **Poetry:** the type of writing found in Psalms and parts of Job.
- **Parable:** brief stories used to bring out a specific truth, like the parables of Jesus.
- **Apocalyptic:** characterized by symbolism and descriptions of visions, as in the books of Revelation and Daniel.

Also, discern whether the author is using *literal* or *figurative* terminology. A *literal* term is one that is to be considered according to its natural or usual meaning. A *figurative* term is symbolic and must be interpreted accordingly. For instance, when Jesus said, "I am the living bread . . . Whoever eats of this bread will live forever" (John 6:51), he was using figurative language. The Jews who heard him interpreted his words literally and asked, "How can this man give us his flesh to eat?" (John 6:52). So it is when you observe and interpret. Unless you observe and understand the nature of the terminology, you may be unfair to the author in your interpretation.

The general tone of a passage is also important. It may be characterized by the mood of joy, thanksgiving, concern, humility, zeal, anger, or despair. The combination of words reveals the writer's feelings.

DISCOVERY SKILLS 2 Bible Focus: 1 Corinthians 13

Practice A—Observe the Details

1. Look for key words.

On page 29 there is a structural diagram of 1 Corinthians 13. Use this passage as practice. Make your observations directly on the page.

First, read the passage and underline what you consider to be some of the key words. Remember that your selections might differ from what others select.

2. Look for other details.

Reread the passage and note the many literary techniques Paul used to convey his message. Note that Paul gives no admonitions in this passage, but he makes strong use of some other approaches.

a) **Cause-and-effect relationships:** See how many examples of these you can find. Remember the little word *if* is one of your clues.

b) **Contrasts:** In this passage there are many contrasts. See how many you can identify. Make your notes in the left margin of the passage. Circle key connectives.

c) **Comparisons and illustrations:** Note their use.

d) **Repetitions and progression of thought:** This passage has several examples of repetition of thought patterns and listing of items. Make note of the repetitions. Study the lists. Is there a progression of thought? Is there a climax?

e) **Description:** Note the positive and negative aspects of love.

f) **Grammatical constructions:** Study the verbs in the passage. What do you note about their tenses? Also note the personal pronouns. When are they used, and when are they not used?

3. Analyze the structure.

Study the verses and bracket those that seem to focus on the same idea. Try to summarize the main idea in each section with a phrase.

Consider also the order that Paul arranges his ideas. Are they arranged logically or psychologically?

1 Corinthians 13

1. If I speak in the tongues of mortals and of angels,
but do have not love,
I am a noisy gong or a clanging cymbal.
2. And if I have prophetic powers,
and understand all mysteries and all knowledge,
and if I have all faith, so as to remove mountains,
but do have not love,
I am nothing.
3. If I give away all my possessions,
and if I hand over my body so that I may boast,
but do not have love
I gain nothing.
4. Love is patient; love is kind;
love is not envious or boastful or arrogant
5. or rude.
It does not insist on its own way;
it is not irritable or resentful;
6. it does not rejoice at wrongdoing,
but rejoices in the truth.
7. It bears all things,
believes all things,
hopes all things,
endures all things.
8. Love never ends.
But as for prophecies, they will come to an end;
as for tongues, they will cease;
as for knowledge, it will come to an end.
9. For we know only in part,
and we prophecy only in part;
10. but when the complete comes,
the partial will come to an end.
11. When I was a child,
I spoke like a child,
I thought like a child,
I reasoned like a child;
when I became an adult,
I put an end to childish ways.
12. For now we see in a mirror, dimly,
but then we will see face to face.
Now I know only in part;
then I will know fully,
even as I have been fully known.
13. And now, faith, hope, and love abide, these three;
and the greatest of these is love.

Practice B—Seek to Know Meanings

1. Ask yourself questions.

While you may be very familiar with this passage, think anew about what Paul means. Ask some *I wonder* questions about the meaning of words and statements:

- Why did Paul say . . . ?
- What is the meaning of . . . ?
- What is the significance of . . . ?
- What is the implication of . . . ?
- What is the relationship between . . . ?

Example

Scripture Passage	Questions for Understanding
1. If I speak in the tongues of mortals and of angels,	Why the emphasis on *mortals* as well as *angels*? Why begin with the conditional clause, "If I . . ."?
but do have not love,	Meaning of *love*?
I am a noisy gong or a clanging cymbal.	Meaning of *noisy gong*? *Clanging cymbal*? Significance of these illustrations? Significance of present tense verb *I am* Relationship between *do not have love* and being a *noisy gong*?

2. Answer questions.

When you ask questions, you stimulate your thinking. Work toward identifying those words, phrases, and statements that need interpretation. You may ask more questions than you can or need to answer. You can select those that seem to be the most relevant. Surely in this passage, the key word *love* must be interpreted. But there are other statements that also need interpreting.

Select some of the questions you asked and seek to answer them by doing some of these things:

- define words
- compare translations
- study cross-references
- wrestle with meanings

In seeking to interpret the message of the chapter, it is important to wrestle with meanings: What is Paul really trying to say about love? Why did he arrange his thoughts in the order he did? Why does he describe both the positive and negative aspects of love?

NOTE: Read Chapter 6, "Ways to Interpret," to gain more detailed information on how to ask questions and how to interpret passages.

Practice C—Personalize Biblical Teachings

When Paul describes love, he approaches it in an impersonal way, "Love is . . ." But everything he says about love has to do with personal relationships. Paul is speaking about a special kind of love—*agape*—a self-giving love that God extends to us through Christ. How can you actualize it in your life?

Evaluation

Are Paul's statements in this chapter valid for relationships today?

Application and Actualization

Review 1 Corinthians 13:4-7. Consider the way Paul describes what love is and what it is not.

1. Think about a situation with conflicts, disagreements, or misunderstandings—a situation in which you have been involved or are now involved.

Present situation: How can you demonstrate these evidences of love as described in 13:4-7? What might be the outcomes?

Previous situation: To what extent did you or did you not demonstrate these evidences of love? What were the results? How might the results have been different?

2. Reflect on a situation in which you need to demonstrate love. Pray about this situation, alone or with others.

NOTE: Read Chapter 13, "Personalizing Biblical Teachings," for a more detailed discussion on how to apply and actualize biblical truths.

5

Studying a Narrative

So far in this study, the focus has been on *discourse literature*—literature that focuses on ideas. You have studied one section of Jesus' Sermon on the Mount and one chapter in an epistle. Both of these passages were didactic in nature; that is, both Jesus and Paul were trying to teach some important concepts.

The Six Guide Words

There is another way of observing a passage: you can use six words as your guides: *who, where, when, what, why, how*. Consider how these words may be used as guides in observing the details of a narrative or story.

Where: Note the setting of a story. It is helpful to locate it on a map.

When: Note the time element in a story. Sometimes you may have to study other passages to determine the time.

Who: Note the characters in a story and how each is described.

What: Note the exact order and details of the events, actions, and conversation of the characters. Sometimes you will find it helpful to list the events, actions, and conversation in chronological order. Note the way characters respond to each other. Read the story imaginatively, trying to build mental images, re-creating the story in your own mind. As you read, try to see, hear, and feel what the characters saw, heard, and felt.

How: Note how the story ends, and how the events and actions of the characters shaped the ending. Note how the characters act and respond to each other.

Why: Ask: Why did these events happen as they did? Why did the characters act and respond as they did? Could they have responded differently?

Approach to a Narrative

It is easy to consider a Bible story superficially. The story may have been heard so many times that it is commonplace. Or the story is thought of only in terms of its message while the period of history when the characters lived is forgotten. Besides using the six guide words, consider these additional approaches in your study.

Be realistic. As you study a Bible story, try to view it in the context of the historical setting of that day. Beware of viewing it through twenty-first century glasses. It is important that you study the laws, the religious teachings, and the customs and practices of those days.

Be imaginative. Most Bible stories tell only the bare facts. As you read a story, give it "flesh and blood" in your imagination. Picture yourself as part of the scene. Visualize what you would be seeing and hearing, including the tone of voices, facial expressions, and body language.

Be empathic. *Empathy* means to identify with other people and their problems and feelings. Try to place yourself in the skin of Bible characters, identifying with them and their emotions, yearnings, hurts, concerns, difficulties, and joys. While it is not difficult to identify with outward actions and responses of Bible characters, try also to determine the inner emotions and needs reflected in the outer actions.

DISCOVERY SKILLS 3 **Bible Focus: Luke 23:32-49**

Practice A—Observe the Details

1. Study Luke 23:32-49.

Practice using these six words as guides for observing details as you concentrate on this very familiar passage in Scripture, one of the accounts of Jesus' crucifixion.

First, read the section quickly and note these things:

- **Where:** Note the places mentioned in the passage.
- **When:** Note the references to time.
- **Who:** Note the people mentioned in the account.
- **What:** Look for some key words in the statements that Jesus and others made.

2. Analyze carefully Luke 23:34-49.

Now make a more careful study of a part of the passage, noting especially how each person responds to Jesus. Divide a sheet of paper into four sections and record the details in chronological order.

Section 1: Record the *whos*—List the persons (other than Jesus) mentioned in the passage.

Section 2: Record *what* they did relating to Jesus.

Section 3: Record *how* they responded to Jesus in terms of what they said. Note the titles they gave him and the pronouns they used relating to Jesus.

Section 4: Record *how* Jesus responded.

WHO (list persons)	WHAT they did	HOW they responded verbally	HOW Jesus responded

Practice B—Seek to Know Meanings

1. Build mental images.

The account of Jesus' crucifixion is a dramatic story. As you study the account, try to imagine what it was like to be there. Re-create in your mind the scene and all the people involved: what they were seeing, hearing, and feeling. Try to imagine the actions, the gestures, and the ways they expressed themselves.

Select one of the persons at the cross and focus on how you think this person spoke and acted.

2. Ask yourself questions.

a) About the words and actions of persons:

- Any significance in the titles the different persons gave Jesus?
- Any significance in the pronouns they used?

b) About key words: One of the key words in this passage is *save*. Note that the leaders, soldiers, and one criminal all use the word. Some questions you might ask yourself are:

- What does the word *save* mean?
- What did it mean to those who were speaking to Jesus?

3. Seek to find answers to questions.

Gain insight into the message of this narrative by doing some of these things:

a) Define words: Look up the word *save* in a dictionary. Think about its meaning and use.

b) Cross-references: Read the account of Jesus' crucifixion in other Gospels. Consider the use of the word *save* in these cross-references: Luke 19:10; John 12:47. What did Jesus mean by the word *save*?

c) Translations: Read other translations to see if you gain additional insight.

Practice C—Personalize Biblical Teachings

The witnesses of the crucifixion reflect the many ways people responded to Jesus. They also can represent how you respond to Jesus at different times in your life.

1. Identify responses.

What kind of responses do the following people reflect:

- soldiers
- leaders
- second criminal
- people
- first criminal
- centurion

2. Identify yourself with a person.

Think about your feelings in a situation you are facing. Identify yourself with one person at the cross who reflects your response to Jesus right now:

- feeling angry because Jesus is not doing what you want him to do
- watching on the sidelines, not getting too involved
- taking Jesus rather casually
- demanding that he "save" your situation
- feeling totally helpless, praying "remember me"
- praising him
- beating your breast

3. Meditate on this scene at the cross.

Complete these statements:

- One thing I can believe is . . .
- One thing I have learned about relationships is . . .
- The good news I find in this scene at the cross is . . .

4. Pray about your response to Jesus.

Invite others to pray with you about your response to Jesus. Pray with them about their response to him.

DISCOVERY SKILLS 4 Bible Focus: Matthew 13:1-9, 18-23 (optional)

Purpose of Bible Study

Hopefully by now you have found that learning these Bible study skills has not been an end in itself, but a means by which you have been enabled to gain deeper insights into the Word of God. But even deeper insights can become ends in themselves unless you have been responding to God's Word with an open and receptive heart.

Studying the Bible is never to be an end in itself, but the means by which you grow in faith and knowledge of God through Jesus Christ. The Bible might be described in two words: *revelation* and *response.* It is a record of God's revelation to all people through Jesus Christ and our response to this revelation. Its purpose is to enable us to come to know this revelation and respond in faith. John's Gospel best describes the purpose of the Bible: "Now Jesus did many other signs in the presence of his disciples, which are not written in this book. But these are written so that you may come to believe that Jesus is the Messiah, the Son of God, and that through believing you may have life in his name" (John 20:30-31).

Since the emphasis in this book is on how to study the Bible, it is appropriate to study Jesus' parable of the sower and the four soils.

Practice A—Observe the Details

1. Read Matthew 13:1-3.

As you read these first three verses, note the *who, where, when,* and *what* of the introduction. Verbs are your clues as to *what* Jesus did.

2. Read Matthew 13:4-9.

As you read the parable, again use the words for insight into the details:

- **Who:** The sower and the seed.
- **Where:** Note the kinds of soil on which the seed fell.
- **What:** Note what happens to the seed in each illustration.
- **How:** Note how the illustration ends in each case in terms of growth of the seed.
- **Why:** Note that in some illustrations Jesus gives a reason (verses 5-6).

3. Read Matthew 13:18-23.

Skip Matthew 13:10-17. Concentrate just on Jesus' interpretation of the parable.

a) **Read this section** and underline about four key words.

b) **Make a special study** of Jesus' interpretation of each of the illustrations. With each illustration do the following:

- **Who:** The who in each illustration. Note how the person responds to the Word.
- **What:** Note what happens to the word that is sown.
- **How:** Note how the illustration ends.
- **Why:** Are there any reasons for the illustration ending as it does?

If you would like to record your observations, you might use the following pattern:

WHO (response to the Word)	**WHAT** happens to the Word	**HOW** the illustration ends	**WHY** (not always given)

Practice B—Seek to Know Meanings

1. Ask questions for understanding.

To guide your questions, you may use:

a) **Definitions:** What are the meanings of some of the key words: *hear, word, understand, bear fruit, good soil,* and so forth.

b) **Relationships:** What is the relationship between *hearing* and *understanding?* What is the relationship between the things that hindered or helped in the growth and the results of the growth?

Ask yourself some additional questions that you think need answering for a deeper understanding of this parable.

2. Interpret your questions.

a) **Use cross-references:** Read Mark 4:14-20 and Luke 8:11-15. Note the additional information and the different ways the ideas are stated in these references.

b) **Compare translations:** Read Matthew 13:18-23 and Luke 8:11-15 in other translations to gain further insight.

c) **Define words and wrestle with meanings:** What does it mean to *hear*? To *understand*? What is the relationship between *hearing* and *understanding*? What is the relationship of *understanding* and *good soil*? What is the meaning of *bears fruit*?

Practice C—Personalize Biblical Teachings

As you think in terms of how to respond to these teachings, summarize what you think Jesus is teaching you in this parable. You might include:

- Anyone can respond in one of these four ways at different times.
- There is a progression in the illustrations, from no response to a great deal of response. The difference between the good soil and the other soils has to do with *perseverance, hanging on,* and *holding fast.*
- God, the sower, is faithful.

Ways to Apply and Actualize

1. **Interpret** this parable in terms of your own experiences.
2. **Complete these statements:**
   - Learning how to study the Bible will help me understand . . .
   - What I receive in this Bible study will depend on . . .
   - Hindrances that prevent the Word of God growing in my life are . . .
   - God's action in my life is . . .
   - The good news I find in this parable for me is . . .
3. **Pray** about your individual response to the Word.

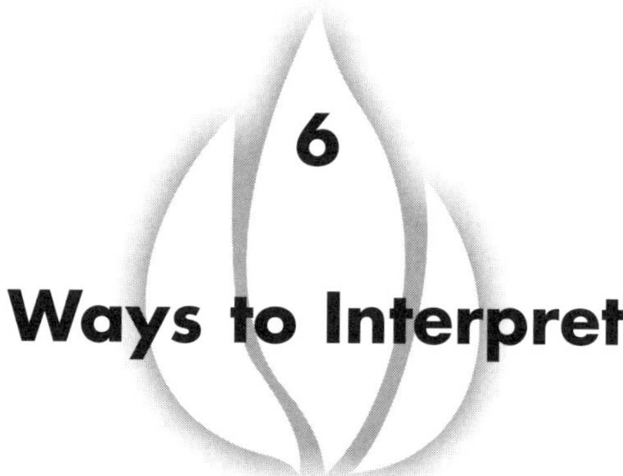

6

Ways to Interpret

While you have been involved already in the process of interpretation in several discovery skills exercises, this chapter will describe the process in more detail.

Purpose of Interpretation

To *interpret* means to explain or tell the meaning of something. When interpreting a scripture passage, aim to determine what the author meant by the words used, keeping in mind the original audience. Try to put yourself in the writer's place and recapture the thoughts, attitudes, and emotions.

The primary purpose of interpretation is to discover what the author meant, to discover the purpose and the message. This is not easy, because the writer is not around anymore. But try to be objective in your interpretations. Don't think about what the passage means to you (this is *application*), but what it seemed to mean to the author. Even so, interpretations will vary a great deal. You can read a dozen commentaries on a biblical passage and have as many different explanations

The Bridge Between Observation and Interpretation

The bridge between observation and interpretation is to ask yourself *questions for understanding*, questions concerning the meaning of words and statements. You probably use this bridge more often than you realize. Usually when you read something, you may read the words in a passage, observe what the words say, and ask questions about words and statements you do not understand. In learning to become a Bible discoverer, you need to do these things deliberately. As you read a passage, always ask questions about meanings.

Why Ask Questions?

Some of the reasons for asking questions are: to stimulate thinking; to force yourself to think seriously about the meaning of words and statements; and to begin to identify those words, phrases, and statements that need interpretation. Asking yourself questions often will lead to more observations, prepare you for application, and serve as the foundation for questions you might use in leading a discussion.

Learning to ask questions about meanings of words is a skill just like learning how to observe. Always remember that you are asking *yourself* the questions for your own understanding. That is why these are called *questions for understanding*, *interpretive* questions, or *I wonder* questions.

What Kind of Questions?

You have been introduced already to the kinds of questions to ask yourself. Now the questions will be considered in greater detail, with suggestions for additional kinds of questions you might ask.

Observing and asking questions are best done simultaneously. Make your observations and ask your questions at the same time, but *do not stop* to answer your questions until you have completed your observations of the passage you are studying. Don't cheat yourself of discoveries by jumping into interpretation too soon.

1. Meaning: What is the meaning of this word, phrase, or statement? How can this word be defined? Is there a deeper meaning in the idea?

2. Significance: What is the significance of a key word, phrase, or statement in the passage? What is its importance to the message? What is the significance of the verb tenses, connectives, and the grammatical constructions? What is the significance of the literary patterns, such as comparisons, contrasts, illustrations, or repetitions? Why has the author used each particular term? Would it make any difference if an idea was left out or stated differently?

3. Implication: What is implied by the use of this term or phrase? What is implied by the use of a question, an illustration, and so forth?

4. Relationship: What is the relationship of words to other words? One part of a verse to another part? Verses to verses? Paragraphs with paragraphs? Chapters with chapters? Relationship of the beginning and end of a chapter or section?

5. Progression: Is there any progression in the thought pattern? Does it move toward a climax? Is one idea built on another? Is there any significance in the order of a series of words or ideas?

6. Literal or figurative: Is this term or statement to be considered literally or figuratively?

This is just a list of possibilities. You probably will never ask all of these questions as you study a passage. As you seek to interpret a passage, you will soon learn to discern which of your questions are relevant and which are not.

When you first begin to ask yourself questions for understanding, you may mix application questions with the interpretive questions. Note the examples of some of the questions you might ask in Matthew 6:25.

- What is the meaning of *worry*?
- What does Jesus mean by *life*?
- What is the significance of the illustrations: *What will we eat?*; *What will we drink?*
- Why shouldn't we worry about life?
- Why shouldn't we be concerned about food and drink?

The first three questions have to do with meanings. The last two have to do with application. While the application questions may come to your mind at the same time as you are thinking about meaning questions, do not write these down. While you focus on the interpretation of a passage, do not allow yourself to think about application. First, discover what Jesus meant by his words. Then you can think about what they mean to you.

Process of Interpretation

Recall that the purpose of interpretation is to discover what the author meant. The purpose of asking questions is to identify those areas that need interpretation. You have already been introduced to some of the approaches in the process of interpretation. Now the approaches will be described in greater detail. They are listed here as steps, although they really do not have to be taken in this order.

Step 1—Pray and Meditate

Only with the guidance of the Holy Spirit can anyone interpret Scripture properly and receive insights into the truths. Prayer and meditation are first in the process of interpretation. Many people have admitted that Bible study was frustrating until they seriously began to pray about their study. After you have observed the details in a passage and asked yourself questions, take some time to meditate prayerfully and thoughtfully on some of the insights you discovered through the process. Give the Lord opportunity to be your interpreter, to guide you in your thinking. An open heart, an open mind, and a spirit of receptivity are hallmarks of a serious Bible student.

Step 2—Discern

While prayer and meditation are important, you need also to use common sense and discernment when seeking meanings. Use discernment as to the validity of some of your questions. Some may overlap and some may be irrelevant. Also weed out any application question—one in which you have used the pronouns *we*, *me*, or *us*. (Why should *we* worry?)

Do not think of answering questions as an end in itself but as a means to gain deeper insight into the whole passage.

Step 3—Define

The dictionary is one of the most important tools of the interpreter. Look up the definitions of the key words in the passage. Also note the synonyms given. Often new insights will come to you as you observe the many variations of meanings that can be applied to a word. Choose the definition that best fits the context of the Bible passage.

When studying definitions, be sure that you relate the definition to the Bible text. Always ask yourself, "What did the author have in mind? What insight into the passage does this definition give me?"

For deeper insight, study the etymology of a word, its root significance and derivation in terms of origin and development through the centuries. Of course, the best way to gain insight into meaning of words is to read a passage in the original Hebrew or Greek, because some words are very difficult to translate into English.

Step 4—Compare

Because of the difficulty scholars have in translating the Bible from the original Hebrew and Greek into English, it is always helpful to compare translations. Compare the standard versions such as *New King James, New American Standard, New International Version, Jerusalem Bible*, and *New Revised Standard Version*. Also consult some of the more "free" translations and paraphrases such as *Phillips, Moffat, Amplified Version, The Living Bible, The Living Translation, Today's English Version, Contemporary English Version.*

Step 5—Investigate

Look for Scripture's own interpretations. Often in the Gospels, Jesus interprets his own statements with explanations and quotations from the Old Testament. Use the margin references and a concordance to find additional references relating to the word or concept that you are considering. You may find many more cross-references than you can use. Select only those that seem to broaden your understanding of the passage.

Step 6—Consult

Books in the Bible were written in a specific historical setting. Be aware of the temptation to evaluate the customs and practices with present-day customs and practices in mind. This is unfair to the writers of the Bible. Consult other resources to gain insight into the historical, cultural, and geographical background of biblical days. Acknowledge that while some customs and standards may not be like contemporary customs or standards, they may reflect universal truths as applicable today as in those days.

Some of the resources to consult are Bible dictionaries, Bible geographies, and atlases. In the study of historical books, such as those found in the Old Testament and the Gospels and Acts in the New Testament, it is especially helpful to locate events on a map and study the customs and culture of those days.

Because of the difficulty of many Bible passages, you may want to consult a commentary, but do it last. If you consult a commentary before your individual study, you deny yourself the joy of discovering truths for yourself. Use the commentary as a tool and not as a crutch.

Step 7—Wrestle

It is possible to follow all of these steps and not come to any definite decisions in terms of the meaning of a verse or passage. Wrestle with the information that you have gained. Think, meditate, evaluate, reflect, and draw conclusions.

Step 8—Summarize

The final step in the process of interpretation is to summarize your conclusions. Summarize insights about individual words or verses as well as about an entire passage. A summary statement might begin with: "therefore, it seems that the author is saying . . . or means . . ." Always remember you are trying to interpret what the author meant.

Recording Your Interpretations

While it is possible to interpret a passage without writing down your findings, you will gain much more in your study if you record your insights. Writing also forces you to be more exact in your analysis and makes it easier to share your findings with others.

One of the best ways is to record your findings according to verses. For instance, if you were recording insights gained in a study of Matthew 6:25-34, you might do the following things with 6:25:

1. **List** the definitions of key words in 6:25 that fit the context of the passage.

2. **Record** phrases from other translations that gave you new insight into 6:25.

3. **List** some of the cross-references you found relating to the key ideas.

4. **Record** any significant information you gained from a Bible dictionary or commentary.

5. **Summarize** what you learned.

7 Studying a Book

One of the aims of this resource is to introduce the steps in discovery Bible study slowly so that you will not become frustrated in the process. Hopefully your skills in observing and interpreting are progressing so that you are ready for the next phase in this study, the expanding phase, in which you study a book. While the focus is the book of James, the main purpose will be to perfect your skills in studying.

Observe the Whole Book

When you begin to study a book in the Bible, read the entire book quickly to get an overview of its contents. Then study it by sections.

Each writer of a book in the Bible had a specific purpose for writing it—certain facts and truths to convey to the readers. The purpose determined the content of the book—what ideas and facts to include and what to omit. The purpose also determined the structure of the book, how the material was arranged. Historical events and situations governed some of the content. The author's own personality and background influenced the literary style.

As you read through a book, observe these major things:

Purpose: What is the author's purpose for writing this book?

Content: What are the major truths and ideas presented to accomplish that purpose?

Structure: How does the material emphasize the purpose?

Literary form: What literary forms are used to bring out the message: prose, poetry, discourse, parable, drama, apocalyptic? When is the terminology literal and when figurative?

Atmosphere: What is the underlying tone of the book? Or parts of the book?

Seek to Discover the Writer and the Writer's Purpose

As you read through a book the first time, focus on the writer and the purpose. No book will carry a detailed description of the writer, but sometimes the writer may disclose some personal information, as Paul often does in his epistles. You can gain insight into a writer's purpose and personality by noting the things that are emphasized, admonitions, convictions, concerns, or illustrations. The writer reveals a purpose in the way the book is structured, the amount of space given to certain topics. This is especially true with the narrative books of the Old Testament and the Gospels and Acts in the New Testament. The writer of the book of Genesis uses 11 chapters to discuss beginnings and 39 chapters to discuss the story of a few persons. What does this suggest to you?

Seek to Discover Facts about the Readers

In some instances, the biblical writers had specific readers in mind. This is especially true of the New Testament epistles. As you read a book the first time, try to discover the original audience. What seems to be their characteristics? Sometimes the writer specifically states problems that the audience was facing, and sometimes they are revealed by the emphasis and the admonitions.

Try to identify with the audience. How would you feel as you read or heard someone else read this letter? In order to identify with these people, you may need to know more about the historical background and culture of their times.

Observe the Structure of the Book

Also in your first reading, see what you can discover about the structure of the book. Some books do not have as definite a structure as others. Keep alert for the way the chapters are grouped according to content. There are a variety of ways a writer can organize and order the material. Consider these ways of ordering content, noting that many books reflect more that one category:

Biographical: in terms of the lives of people. Genesis is an example, with some material organized according to the lives of Abraham, Isaac, Jacob, and Joseph.

Historical: in terms of succession of events. Exodus is an example, with material organized according to the experiences of the Israelites as they fled Egypt.

Chronological: in terms of the time when events happened. Both Genesis and Exodus contain examples of this type of organization, where the story is told in chronological order.

Geographical: in terms of the places where the events happened. Exodus is also geographical in arrangement in that the places as well as the events are emphasized.

Logical or ideological: in terms of the ideas themselves. The prophetical books and the epistles are examples of these types of arrangements. Romans is fairly logical in structure, whereas Philippians is ideological, organized according to ideas but not necessarily in a logical sequence.

Focus on Smaller Sections

After you have read the entire book, begin to focus on one section at a time. Usually you begin with the first paragraph of the first chapter. But wherever you begin, it is important that you see the section in the context of the whole book.

DISCOVERY SKILLS 5

**Bible Focus:
The Book of James,
James 3:6-12**

Practice A—Read the Book of James

1. Observe the writer and readers.

Before you begin to read the book of James, divide a sheet of paper in half. Title the left half of the sheet, "The author: characteristics, convictions, and concerns." Title the right half, "The readers: their characteristics, problems, and concerns."

As you read, jot down things you learn about the author and the audience from what the author says. Don't go into too much detail.

2. Summarize purpose.

After this first reading, try to summarize in a few statements what you think is the author's purpose for writing this book.

3. Consider the structure of James.

Does the structure appear to be biographical, historical, chronological, geographical, or ideological? Someone has said that the book of James is more like a sermon, the kind that was preached in his day. Some scholars suggest that it might have been a sermon that was later put into writing. How does your observation of the structure agree or disagree with this?

4. Consider the author.

There are different opinions on the authorship of the book of James. Read in a commentary or Bible dictionary the various views of the authorship of James.

Practice B—Observe Details of James 3:6-12

1. Review.

You already have had several practices in observing the details in passages. You will continue to develop these skills in this practice. Begin with one of the paragraphs in the center of the book, James 3:6-12. Review the suggestions on how to observe: the short list in Chapter 3 and the more detailed list in Chapter 4.

2. Read thoughtfully.

As you begin to study this passage, do so prayerfully and thoughtfully: praying that the Holy Spirit will guide you in your reading. Consider the first verse and the way you might think about it as you read: "And the tongue is a fire. The tongue is placed among our members as a world of iniquity; it stains the whole body, sets on fire the cycle of nature, and is itself set on fire by hell" (James 3:6).

As you read the words in the first sentence, note that the key words are *tongue* and *fire*. This is a comparison, the tongue is called *a fire*. Also note that the verb is present tense. As you make note of these things, you might begin asking yourself some *I wonder* questions. Reading on, note other statements, words, and phrases about which you may wonder.

Remember that the questions you ask yourself at this point are *questions for understanding*.

3. Observe and record deliberately.

As you continue to study this section of James, record your observations of words, phrases, and wonderings on paper. Divide a sheet of paper horizontally into three equal sections. Title the sections as follows:

Observations	Scripture Passage	Questions for Understanding

In the center section, write down portions of the scripture passage in sequence. It is best to copy parts of a verse at a time, rather than a whole verse, but always include a unit of words such as a phrase or clause that has a unified idea. Note how the Bible passages are arranged on page 52.

In the left section, record your observations. In the right section, record the questions you ask yourself about meanings.

Note the example on page 52. When recording observations, it is helpful to underline words and phrases taken from Scripture. The words that would be underlined are in italics on page 52. Be more detailed in your observations. At first, you may have difficulties in knowing what to say about words and phrases, but practice will develop your powers of observation. The example focuses on 3:6-8. Continue with 3:9-12.

Practice C—Seek to Know Meanings

1. Select some key questions

After making a thorough study of James 3:6-12, you may have asked many more questions than you have time to answer—or are even relevant to the message of the passage. Select just a few to investigate.

2. Interpret some of your questions

Review Chapter 6 on interpretation, especially the section on how to record interpretation (page 45) Follow those suggestions as you seek to interpret some of the words or statements in this passage.

Observations	Scripture Passage	Questions for Understanding
6. *tongue* and *fire*—keywords. comparison—tongue with fire. *is*—present-tense verb.	James 3:6 And the tongue is a fire.	Meaning of *tongue*? Why is the tongue called a fire? Does the present-tense verb imply tongue always is a fire? Why not "like a fire"? Would meaning be the same?
second comparison—*tongue* with *world*. *is*—another present-tense verb; *iniquity*: describes the kind of world. *among our members*: describes place.	The tongue is placed among our members as a world of iniquity;	Meaning of *world of iniquity*? Meaning of *among our members*?
stains—shows action of tongue; *whole*—describes the extent of influence of body.	it stains the whole body,	Significance of *stains*? How can the tongue stain the whole body? Meaning of *body*?
sets on fire—another action of tongue. *cycle of nature*—describes what is set on fire.	sets on fire the cycle of nature,	Meaning of *cycle of nature*? How can the tongue influence the cycle of nature?
The tongue is acted upon. It sets things on fire and is set on fire—reveals source of fire.	and is itself set on fire by hell.	Significance of this statement? Does James really mean that the tongue is set on fire by hell?
7. *for*: key connective, implies a reason. Introduces an illustration. *every species*: inclusive, all kinds of animals mentioned. *can be tamed*: implies possibilities. *has been tamed*: describes what has happened in past.	7. For every species of beast and bird, or reptile and sea creature, can be tamed and has been tamed by the human species,	Why this illustration? Why such an inclusive statement? Meaning of word *tamed*? Significance of *human species*?
8. *but*: key connective, brings out contrast as to what anyone can do with animals, even savage ones, but not with his or her tongue. Again emphasis on word *tame*.	8. but no one can tame the tongue—	Significance of words *no one*? Does this imply that God can do what human beings cannot do?
Note descriptive words about tongue, words that can be used to describe animals.	a restless evil, full of deadly poison.	Significance of these descriptive words? Relationship of verses 7 and 8 with verse 6?

As reminders, here are some things to do:

a) **State your questions.**

b) **Define some key words.** Use a dictionary.

c) **Read translations.** Record parts of the translation that give you insight into meanings.

d) **Look up cross-references.** Copy the verses that provide additional insight.

f) **Study other resources.** You may need to read a commentary or other resources for information about some difficult statements.

g) **Wrestle with meanings and summarize.** Consider what you have been learning and formulate a statement summarizing what you think the author was saying.

Practice D—Personalize Biblical Teachings

1. Evaluation

Is this description of the tongue a true description? What is the significance of the present tenses of the verbs? Do we always have the power to choose what our tongues will do?

2. Application

Complete some of these statements:

- One time when I experienced the power of the tongue to bless or to burn was . . .
- One time when I learned how the use of my tongue can "stain my body" was . . .
- The greatest difficulty I have with my tongue is . . .

3. Actualization

1. **Discuss** how the use of your tongue can help or hinder your relationships.

2. **Use** your tongue to bless by sharing with the others what you admire about them.

3. **Reflect** on any problems you may have with your tongue and pray about your concerns.

DISCOVERY SKILLS 6 **Bible Focus: James 3:1-5**

Practice A—Observe and Record Details

After you have completed a study of James 3:6-12, do a similar study of James 3:1-5. Divide a sheet of paper in three sections and title them as follows:

Observations	Scripture Passage	Questions for Understanding

In the center section, copy units of thought from James 3:1. Record your observations in the left section and your questions for understanding in the right section. In this passage note the admonitions, warnings, reasons for doing things, conditional clause and results, illustrations, comparisons, emphatic statements. Also note carefully the verb tenses.

Practice B—Seek to Know Meanings

Strive to interpret the verses you observed, following the same pattern. Record your findings.

1. **Select** some of the key questions.

2. **Define** some of the key words.

3. **Compare** translations.

4. **Study** cross-references, noting especially Luke 6:43-45.

5. **Consult** some resources to learn more about the position of teachers in the days of James.

6. **Wrestle** with the meanings of the comparisons made and summarize your conclusions.

Practice C—Personalize Biblical Teachings

Study James 3:1-5 and 6-12 together because they are a unified thought on the serious responsibility of being a teacher.

1. Evaluation

Consider what James is saying about the tongue and people in leadership. How do you react to the following statements:

- People in leadership are subject to greater judgment and criticism.
- If a person can control the tongue, he or she can control the whole body.

2. Application

How would you apply Luke 6:43-45 to James 3:1-5? How can our tongues be controlled?

3. Creative Expression

Reflect on one of your insights in a creative way: make a poster illustration; make a montage of pictures; write a poem, song, prayer, or devotional; or do something else you enjoy. Share what you do with others.

8

Observing the Whole

One danger in Bible study is to get lost in the single phrases and verses of a Bible passage and never understand the entire message the author was trying to communicate. Beware of observing words and phrases as ends in themselves, no matter how interesting or meaningful they may be. Observe the words and phrases in relation to the whole sentence, the whole paragraph, and the whole chapter. In order to understand the whole, learn how to analyze the structure of a scriptural passage—observing how the author has arranged the material.

Definition of Structure

The term *structure* refers to the underlying design, framework, skeleton, organization, or arrangement of material. Anything that is planned with a specific purpose will have structure, whether it is a building, a car, a piece of music, a watch, or a literary composition. The function of a thing determines its form. Insight into its design and structure helps to better understand its purpose.

Compare the process of observing the structure of a Bible passage to observing a new house. Imagine that friends invite you to see their new house. When you arrive, construction materials are scattered all over the yard. There are window frames and windows, the doors, the walls, and the bricks. Your friends ask, "How do you like our new house?" You probably would reply, "I see the parts that make up a house, but I still don't know what your house looks like."

So it is in Bible study. It is not enough just to see the parts, or even understand the parts. You need to see the parts in relation to the whole before you can grasp the entire message.

Observing Structure Through a Diagram

One of the best ways to analyze a passage is to make a structural diagram of it. In chapters 3 and 4 there are examples of structural diagrams of Matthew 6:25-34 and 1 Corinthians 13. Review these as you consider the following suggestions for making a structural diagram:

1. Copy the units of phrases and clauses in the center of a page, separating the units so that they have the most meaning to you.

2. Line up major clauses and ideas so that the key ideas can be seen easily.

3. Place modifying phrases and clauses under the words they describe, but don't break up the thought pattern too much.

4. Place series of words, phrases, clauses, parallel thoughts, and parallel constructions under one another.

Value of Structural Diagram

There is no right or wrong way to set up a structural diagram. Any way that makes sense to you will have value. The very process of doing it enables you to gain deeper insight into the passage, especially if you are studying a difficult passage. Once you get the ideas in front of you in some graphic form, it is easier to see the key ideas and relationships of the parts to the whole.

Analyze Your Structural Diagram

After you have arranged the units of thought of a passage in a graphic way, analyze its contents by doing some of these things:

1. Study the verses and bracket those that seem to be on the same topic.

2. Summarize the main thought or emphasis in each group of verses and write your summary in the left margin. Try to summarize using just a phrase or even one word.

3. Identify key words and ideas by underlining and circling them. You might want to use colored pencils to highlight ideas. Circle key connectives.

4. Use arrows and lines to show relationships, repeated words, and other things you observe.

5. In the left margin, record other observations: commands, warnings, conditional clauses, reasons and results, comparisons, contrasts, and grammatical constructions.

6. In the right margin, list some of your questions for understanding, based on your observations.

DISCOVERY SKILLS 7 **Bible Focus: James 3**

Practice A—Consider Diagrams

1. Analyze diagrams.

On page 59 there is a structural diagram of James 3:1-12. Note how the diagram is constructed. If you diagramed the passage, you might arrange the unit of thoughts differently. This is just one example.

Study the diagram and bracket the verses that seem closely related in emphasis. In the left margin summarize each grouping in a brief statement.

2. Make a structural diagram.

Read James 3:13-18 and make a structural diagram of this paragraph. Follow the suggestions on page 57. Make your diagram in the center of the page, allowing margins. Try to get the entire diagram on one page; type, if possible. If you place your diagram in the center of a horizontal sheet, you will have more margin space, but you may have to use two sheets.

3. Analyze your diagram.

Bracket those verses that seem to focus on one idea. Summarize each grouping in a brief statement. Using a colored pencil, underline and circle key words, connectives, and ideas. In the left margin, record what you observe, noting admonitions, contrasts, conditional clauses, descriptive words, and series of ideas. In the right margin, list your questions for understanding.

Practice B—Seek to Know Meanings

Interpret verses you have observed in James 3:13-18, following the pattern that you have used in your previous studies. Record your findings.

1. Select one or two of your key questions.

2. Define some of the key words, especially the term *wisdom*.

3. Compare translations.

4. Study cross-references, especially some relating to wisdom.

5. Consult other resources.

6. Wrestle with information that you gained in your study. Summarize your conclusions in some brief statements.

Structural Diagram—James 3:1-12

1. Not many of you become teachers, my brothers and sisters,
for you know that we who teach
will be judged with greater strictness.
2. For all of us make many mistakes.
Anyone who makes no mistakes
in speaking
is perfect,
able to keep the whole body
in check with a bridle.
3. If we put bits into the mouths of horses
to make them obey us,
we guide their whole bodies.
4. Or look at ships:
though they are so large
that it takes strong winds to drive them,
yet they are guided by a very small rudder
wherever the will of the pilot directs.
5. So also the tongue is a small member,
yet it boasts of great exploits.
How great a forest is set ablaze by a small fire!
6. And the tongue is a fire.
The tongue is placed among our members
as a world of iniquity;
it stains the whole body,
sets on fire the cycle of nature,
and is itself set on fire by hell.
7. For every species of beast and bird,
of reptile and sea creature,
can be tamed and
has been tamed by the human species,
8. but no one
can tame the tongue—
a restless evil, full of deadly poison.
9. With it we bless the Lord and Father,
and with it we curse those
who are made in the likeness of God.
10. From the same mouth
come blessing and cursing.
My brothers and sisters, this ought not to be so.
11. Does a spring pour forth
from the same opening both fresh and brackish water?
12. Can a fig tree, my brothers and sisters, yield olives,
or a grapevine figs?
No more can salt water yield fresh.

Practice C—Personalize Biblical Teachings

Now that you have studied Chapter 3 of James, consider the relationship of the three paragraphs with each other. In terms of key words, the paragraphs might be summarized in three words: *teachers, tongue, wisdom.*

1. Evaluation

How would you compare James 3:13-18 and 1 Corinthians 13?

2. Application and Actualization

a) **Meditate** on James 3:17-18. How might the statements in these verses be a pattern for demonstrating "true wisdom" in your Bible study group? In your home relationships? Describe specific examples.

b) **Complete** the statements:

- When trying to demonstrate "true wisdom," my greatest problem is . . .
- The good news I find in James 3 is . . .

c) **Reflect** on a subject or issue for which you need more wisdom. Pray concerning your needs.

9

Summarizing Through Charts

When you study longer sections of Scripture, it is not always possible to copy every word in a passage. You need to abbreviate the process through the use of charts. In a chapter, instead of copying every word, you can summarize the key ideas on a horizontal or vertical chart.

Horizontal Chart

To make a horizontal chart, construct the chart lengthwise on a sheet of paper. (See example on page 63.) Draw a line across the page. Block off as many divisions, both above and below the main line, as there are paragraphs in the chapter. The divisions might even be in proportion to the size of the paragraphs, with more space for the longer paragraphs and less for the shorter ones.

Title the paragraphs according to the content. Place your titles above the main line. In the sections below the line, list the main ideas found in each paragraph. Bracket the paragraphs that seem to be on the same topic.

Vertical Chart

This type of chart is constructed vertically on a sheet of paper. (See example on page 63.) Draw a large rectangle and block out the divisions according to the paragraphs. Vertical charts work best for shorter portions of material. The vertical chart is very good to use when you want to study the relationship of ideas within paragraphs and between paragraphs. Bracket paragraphs that seem to focus on the same ideas and record summary titles in the margins outside the chart.

Value of Charts

Charting a passage has value as the charting process:

- Forces you to think structurally about the material in a passage.
- Helps you see the major ideas.
- Helps you see relationships between paragraphs.
- Helps you identify ideas that are emphasized.
- Helps you to summarize ideas.
- Helps you see everything in context.

DISCOVERY SKILLS 8 Bible Focus: James 3 and 1

Practice A—Vertical Chart of James 3

Since you have already studied the different paragraphs in James 3, summarize the teachings in this chapter with a vertical chart. Draw a rectangle in the center of a sheet of paper. Divide the rectangle into three sections according to the paragraphs. List the major ideas in each paragraph. Place in the left margin a summary title for each paragraph. Try to indicate the relationship between the paragraphs. What is the relationship between the paragraph on teachers, the one on the tongue, and the one on wisdom?

verses 1-5
verses 6-12
verses 13-18

Practice B—Horizontal Chart of James 1

1. Read James 1.

There are two ways to set up a horizontal chart for this chapter. One is to construct it according to paragraphs. The other is to construct it according to the main divisions.

According to the paragraphs: This is the kind of chart you can make when you first read a chapter. Until you study the chapter, you do not know what the main divisions are. One of the problems of this kind of chart is that the spaces may become so small that you are limited in your recording.

Chart of James 1 according to paragraphs:

List titles for each paragraph above the horizontal line.

verses 1-4	verses 5-8	verses 9-11	verses 12-15	verses 16-18	verses 19-21	verses 22-25	verses 26-27

List main ideas about each paragraph below the horizontal line.

Title your paragraphs according to their content. Place your titles in the spaces above the line. In the sections below the line, summarize the main ideas in each paragraph. Note the admonitions, reasons, results, and promises.

Example of how to summarize James 1:1-4:

Accept trials as friends 1 4
Greetings Count trials as joy Produces endurance Endurance makes you mature and complete

According to major divisions: In this type of chart the paragraphs are listed under the main divisions and you have more space to record.

Chart of James 1 according to divisions:

verses 1-3 verses 2-4 verses 5-8 verses 9-11	verses 12-15 verses 16-18	verses 19-21 verses 22-25 verses 26-27

Bracket paragraphs on the same topic. Here are some possible titles for the groupings that are suggested by marks on the chart:

- **James 1:1-11** Admonitions relating to trials
- **James 1:12-18** Admonitions relating to temptations
- **James 1:19-27** Admonitions relating to the Word

Practice C—Study One Paragraph

After you have made a summary chart of James 1, showing an overview of the major teachings, study each paragraph more thoroughly. To practice, concentrate on just one paragraph. Make a thorough study of this paragraph, using the skills you have been learning. Here are the steps to follow:

1. Select one paragraph.

2. Observe its contents.

Follow the pattern you have been using.

Observations	Scripture	Questions for Understanding
	(Make a structural diagram like the one you made with James 3:13-18. You may use more than one page.)	

3. Select a few key questions for interpretation.

Follow the process you have been using when interpreting statements in a passage: define words; compare translations; look up one or two cross-references; wrestle with meaning; summarize. Some of the statements in this chapter are difficult to interpret, and you may need to study a commentary to get someone else's insight.

4. Consider some ways you might personalize the truths in the paragraph.

Think how you might apply and actualize one of the truths in a real-life situation. You might use this pattern:

- One thing I can believe is . . .
- One thing I am encouraged to do is . . .
- One thing this passage teaches about relationships is . . .
- The good news in this passage that meets one of my needs is . . .

10

More about Interpretation

One of the first and very important aspects of interpretation is the study of key words in the passage. This chapter focuses in detail on the things you might do in the study of key words.

Use of Dictionary

The dictionary is one of the most important tools a Bible discoverer needs to use. Here are some of the uses of the dictionary.

Definitions: The most common use of the dictionary is to study the definitions of a word. Usually there are several from which to choose, and you must select those that best fit the context of the passage.

Synonyms: Select those that best fit the context of the passage. Sometimes it is helpful to look up the definitions of some of the synonyms in order to gain a clearer understanding of a key word. Even studying some of the antonyms can be helpful.

Examples: In larger dictionaries, there often are examples of the usage of a word. Many times you can find an example relating to a religious or theological use. These too can add insight into meanings.

Etymology of word: This is the study of word origins and development through the centuries. Most large dictionaries include etymology of a word, usually in brackets after the pronunciation of the word. The key to the abbreviations used usually is found in the front of the dictionary. The word that comes first within the brackets is usually the most recent form of the word.

Use of Translations

As you seek to interpret a passage, be mindful that an English version is always one step removed from the original language of Hebrew or Greek. In many cases it has been very difficult for translators to find English words equivalent to the original Hebrew or Greek. The best way to find the true definition of a word is to read a passage in the original language. For those who cannot read Hebrew or Greek, it is helpful to read a passage in several translations to see the various ways a word can be translated. There are some translations, such as the *Amplified Version* of the Bible, that provide a variety of ways a word might be translated.

Use of Cross-References

You can gain insight into meaning of words by studying other cross-references in which the word is used. With the use of a concordance, you can find many biblical references to a word. Select only those that fit the context of the passage.

Use of Other Resources

Sometimes you need the help of other scholars to understand a word. You can find such help in a Bible dictionary, Bible encyclopedia, or a commentary. Most Bible study resources are available in electronic versions, making it possible to conduct thorough searches for information very quickly.

DISCOVERY SKILLS 9 **Bible Focus: James 2**

Practice A—Be on the Alert for Details

1. Study James 2:1-7.

As you observe a passage, be alert to what you can learn about the author and the original readers:

- Try to imagine what the author saw, heard, and felt. Select words that reveal feelings.
- Note the use of questions and how they are answered.
- Note the contrasts.

2. Study James 2:8-13.

Underline some of the key words, note the conditional clauses and the results suggested, and note the admonitions and warnings.

3. Study James 2:14-26.

Underline some of the key words, count how many times *faith* and *works* is used, and note questions and how they are answered.

Practice B—Seek to Know Meanings

1. Study key words.

There are many things that need interpretation in this chapter, such as the relationship of the rich and the poor in 2:1-7; and the meaning of the words *law, royal law, whole law,* and *law of liberty* in 2:8-13. If you have the time, investigate these words, but concentrate mainly on the key words in James 2:14-26: *faith, works, believe, justified.* Define the words using a dictionary, other translations, cross-references, and other Bible study resources.

2. Summarize insights in a visual way.

Summarize your insights in a paragraph, but also express them visually. Illustrate your concept of the relationship between *faith* and *works* through a poster, diagram, illustration, or picture, using symbols, words, pictures, circles, squares, lines, colors—anything that expresses visually your concept of what James is saying.

11

More about Charts and Summarization

Importance of Summarization

Summaries help crystallize major teachings and are an aid to memory. A summary should reveal both content and arrangement of the Bible passage. Keep the parts related to the whole:

- Relate verses to the whole paragraph.
- Relate paragraphs to the whole chapter.
- Relate chapters to the whole book.
- Relate individual truths to the whole message.

Previous chapters have focused on the use of structural diagrams and charts in order to analyze material and summarize content. This chapter reviews and expands the use of charts, outlines, and diagrams in Bible study.

General Ways to Summarize

1. Book chart: When studying a book, make a horizontal chart, blocking off a space for each chapter. Give a title to each chapter. Group the chapters into divisions according to similarity in content. Title the divisions. List the main teachings and the main characteristics of the book.

2. Chapter chart: When studying a chapter, make a horizontal or vertical chart for each chapter, allowing space for each paragraph. Give each paragraph a factual or interpretive title. List the main teachings in each paragraph. Group the paragraphs according to their similarity in emphasis. Refer to Practice B in Chapter 9, "Summarizing through Charts," for examples of this.

3. Paragraph chart: Chart or diagram the main teachings in any paragraph that demands special study. Refer to Practice C in Chapter 9, "Summarizing through Charts," for an example of this.

4. Topical chart: If your Bible study is topical, make a chart to show the various aspects of your topic. For example, if you were considering the topic of prayer, you might chart your findings under these headings: prayer admonitions; prayer promises; conditions for answered prayers.

5. Outline: List the main and subordinate points in a logical or topical outline. While outlines have their value, they are not as visual as a chart.

6. Brief statement: Summarize the author's purpose or the content of a paragraph or chapter in a brief phrase or statement.

7. Paraphrase: Write the content of a paragraph in your own words. Follow the text, but paraphrase it in contemporary language.

8. Summary diagram: Show the relationship of ideas in a visual way.

Summary Diagrams

The term *structural diagram*, as used earlier, describes a way to arrange the units of thought in a paragraph so that it is easier to observe the structure and content of the paragraph. A *summary diagram* is an arrangement of ideas to show their relationship to each other. In the *structural diagram* you wrote down all of the words in a paragraph. In a *summary diagram* you list only the principal ideas that you seek to analyze. It differs from an outline in that it is more informal. It differs from a chart in that it is not boxed by lines.

Reread James 1:26-27. The content of these verses can be analyzed according to their relationships. The summary diagram is a simple way to place the truths of a passage in a graphic form. For example:

Theme: Tests of religion: People who consider themselves religious:

Test	*Situation*	*Results*
Do not bridle their tongues	Deceive their hearts	Their religion is worthless
Care for orphans and widows, keep unstained	Honest with self and God	Pure religion

Summary diagrams may be done in visual and graphic ways using things other than words, such as symbols, lines, circles, arrows, or squares. The purpose is to help you visualize the key teachings of a verse or passage in order to better understand them.

Summarization by Means of Charts

The chart is one of the most effective ways to enable you to grasp the whole picture of a chapter or book. It has real value as a study device and as a teaching tool.

Study chart: The purpose of a study chart is to record the observations you make as you study a portion of Scripture. In some chapters, you may want to trace what each paragraph teaches about certain ideas. You can make a horizontal chart, blocking off as many sections as paragraphs. As you concentrate on each paragraph, list the major teachings, concepts of God, attitudes toward God, or key phrases. Even though you may find many things you would like to record, limit your chart to one or two pages. A chart loses its value if it covers too many pages.

Summary chart: While your study chart may be very detailed, your summary chart should be simple and concise. From your study chart, sift out most of the details and keep only the key ideas. The purpose of the summary chart is to make a bird's-eye view of the principal teachings in a passage. Your study chart will be factual in nature, while your summary chart might be interpretive as well as factual.

Teaching chart: A teaching chart is one that is placed on a board or displayed on an easel to help learners gain insight into the key ideas of a passage. Encourage learners to help you develop the teaching chart. Include whatever is necessary to convey the message and structure of a passage.

What to Include in a Chart

- Main divisions of a chapter or book
- Theme, titles of paragraphs or chapters
- Key words, phrases, key ideas, verses
- Relationships: comparisons, contrasts, repetitions, cause and effect, progression of ideas
- Perspective: relationship of chapters
- Proportion: amount of space given to major topics
- Arrangement of material: geographical, biographical, chronological, psychological, ideological
- Characteristics of chapters and books
- Topical studies: teachings about God, people, sin, redemption
- Literary features: quotable passages, figures of speech

What to Consider When Making a Chart

- Make ideas easy to see at a glance.
- Avoid making it too large or too detailed. If you have a lot of information, break it down into several charts.
- Condense your information into words and phrases.
- Emphasize the major ideas.
- Reflect your own insights.

Note the sample chart on page 73.

Example of Horizontal Chart: Book of James

Theme: Living faith is revealed through active works
Key words: Faith, works, doers.
Key verses: 2:17, 26. "So faith by itself, if it has no works, is dead."

Perfection of Faith	Proof of Faith	Practical Evidence of Faith		Power of Faith
Chapter 1. Through trials	Chapter 2. Through works	Chapter 3. Through wisdom	Chapter 4. Through attitudes	Chapter 5. Through perseverance
1. Salutation. 2. Possibilities of trials (2-11). Purpose (2:4) Guidance (5-8) Strength (9-11) 3. Possibilities of temptations. (12-18) Source (12-15) Contrast (16-18) 4. Power of the Word. (19-27)	1. Faith demands works. (1-13) 2. Faith worthless without works. (14-17) 3. Works the proof of faith. (18-26) Examples: Abraham, Rahab	1. Faith expressed through right use of tongue. (1-12) Possibilities Characteristics 2. Faith expressed through wisdom. (13-18)	1. Faith expressed through right attitudes. (1-12) toward world toward God toward neighbor 2. Faith expressed through reliance on God. (13-17)	1. Patience in suffering. (1-11) 2. Honest in speech. (12) 3. Perseverance in prayer. (13-20)

Characteristics of the book of James:
Practical rather than doctrinal.
Emphasis on moral and social living.
Many exhortations.

Lessons:
1. Let trials perfect your character.
2. Show your faith in deeds of love.
3. Beware of the uncontrolled tongue.
4. Pray!

Example of Vertical Chart: James 4

Theme: Faith revealed through proper attitudes

Source of Problems	
	(verses 1-6) Problems—disputes and conflicts Reasons: Because of wrong attitude Ruled by evil desires Because of wrong relationships Friendship with world Enmity with God
	(verses 7-10)
	(verses 11-12)
	(verses 13-17)

DISCOVERY SKILLS 10 **Bible Focus: James 4**

Practice A—Make a Vertical Chart of James 4

Read James 4 and make a summary vertical chart of the contents of the chapter. On page 74 you will find the beginning of the chart. Complete it by summarizing the content of each section with some concise statements. In the left margin, place a summary title for each section.

Practice B—Focus on Smaller Section

1. Thorough study of one paragraph.

Select one paragraph and make a thorough study as you have done in previous chapters

a) Use observation form:

Observations	Diagram of passage	Questions for Understanding

b) Select a few key questions for interpretation.

c) Share how one of the key ideas in this passage might be applied and actualized in your life.

2. Short study.

Select one of the key verses and use the following form for consideration.

Verses	Interpretation	Actualization
Observations about the verses	Insights gained through defining words, comparing translations, looking at one cross-reference	Ways I can actualize the truths of these verses in my life.

Practice C—Personalize Biblical Teachings

As you reflect on ways to apply and actualize some of the statements in this chapter, consider some of the following suggestions.

1. Discuss the following statement.

"Desire is the root of all the evils that ruin and divide people." Do you agree or disagree? Why?

2. Study the key exhortations in James 4:7-10.

Is there any significance in their order? How would you carry out some of these exhortations? Give illustrations.

3. Read James 4 prayerfully.

As you read ask yourself these questions:

- For what special area in my life is the Lord speaking to me personally in this chapter?
- What are some prayers of thanksgiving, confession, petition, and intercession for me to pray?

DISCOVERY SKILLS 11

Bible Focus: James 5, The Book of James

For some time you have been studying the book of James. You have been observing, asking questions, interpreting, diagramming, charting, summarizing, analyzing, and applying. All Bible skills are means to an end: to discover the message in God's Word. Now that you are coming to the close of your study, ask yourself: "What has the Lord revealed to me personally through the study in James? What are the evidences that my faith is a living faith revealed through the fruit and works in my life?"

Practice A—Study James 5

1. Make a horizontal chart of James 5.

Title each paragraph and list the important ideas in each paragraph.

2. Read James 5 prayerfully.

Spend some time meditating on one aspect in the chapter. Express your thoughts in some devotional way: in a song, a poem, a prayer, or a devotional thought.

3. Make a special study of James 5:13-16.

Key observations	Interpretation of some of the key ideas	One way I can actualize the teachings in this passage

Practice B—Review the Book of James

1. Make a chart.

Make a horizontal or vertical chart or summary diagram reflecting the main teachings in the letter of James.

On page 73 there is a chart showing some of the general teachings in the book. Let your chart or diagram reflect what you consider the most important teachings.

2. Study a theme.

Select one of the themes in James (suffering, temptations, tongue, prayer, faith, and works) and make a special study, reflecting observations, interpretation, and application.

3. Team project.

Team with one other person to plan some way to involve others in some aspect or teaching in James.

a) Select a hymn that reflects a teaching in James to sing with a group.
b) Write words to a familiar tune or compose music for one of the passages in James to sing together.
c) Present some imaginary conversation with James on an issue.
d) Provide some open-ended or true-or-false statements for discussion.
e) Apply some teaching in James to present-day problems through the use of newspaper clippings, pictures, cartoons, or advertisements.

Practice C—Evaluation

1. Some teachings in James that have strengthened my faith are . . .

2. One way the study of James has changed my attitudes or actions is . . .

3. Some of the study skills I have found most helpful are . . .

4. Some of the frustrations I had are . . .

5. Ways I have already used the skills or can use them are . . .

12

Studying a Longer Book

Whether you are studying a paragraph or a whole book, the basic approach to Bible study is the same. Here is a review of the general procedures.

1. **Observe** exactly what the writer is saying.

2. **Interpret** carefully what the author has written, gaining insight into the meanings.

3. **Summarize** concisely, setting forth the major teachings in the passage, chapter, or book.

4. **Evaluate** fairly, determining the relevance of the biblical teachings to present-day living.

5. **Apply** personally in order to make the biblical teachings meaningful in your own life.

6. **Actualize** your convictions. Put into action the challenges you find in your study.

These steps are basic, but the manner to apply the steps will be determined by the amount of material to cover, the purpose of your study, and the time you have. This chapter presents ways to apply these skills to longer books of the Bible

Procedure in the Study of a Gospel

These steps show how to use discovery Bible study skills to approach the study of a longer book, using Mark as an example.

Step 1: Observe the Whole Book

1. Skim through the book of Mark quickly: observe the general content and grouping of material.

2. As you read the Gospel the second time, prepare a horizontal chart, blocking out 16 spaces across your sheet, one space for each chapter. As you read each chapter, summarize its content in a brief phrase or title and write this in the chapter space.

As you read, note the relationship of the chapters to each other. Bracket together chapters related to specific phases of Jesus' life, such as his preparation, ministry, sufferings and death, and resurrection. When you have finished reading the book, you should have before you a summary of the whole book, showing general chapter content and the main structure of the book.

Step 2: Observe the Chapters

The second step is to carefully study the individual chapters. Again, it is very helpful to block out the material in chart form. Sketch a horizontal chart for each chapter and allow as many spaces as there are paragraphs. Title your paragraphs by summarizing the main thought of each paragraph into a short phrase. Study the paragraphs to see which are on the same topic. Bracket these together. Note how the paragraphs are tied together and their relationship to each other.

In the study of each chapter there are many features you can record on your chart:

1. Make note of key persons, places, events, ideas, characteristics of people, the actions of people, and their reactions and attitudes.

2. Keep in mind the patterns of literary structure as described in Chapter 4. Make note of significant repetitions, comparisons, contrasts, centers of interest, progressions of ideas, and climax. Note whether there are contrasts, repetition of ideas, or progression of ideas between paragraphs.

3. Note how the message of the portion is emphasized: Through a parable? Narrative? Question? Quotations? Story? Conversation?

4. Note the atmosphere. How would you describe it? Is it controversial? Tense? Challenging? Peaceful?

5. Study the reaction of the persons to each other and to Jesus. Especially note those who oppose him, reasons for opposition, and methods used against him.

6. Make a special study of the miracles of Jesus and of his discourses.

7. Discover what the chapter teaches about four main concepts of the Bible: God, people, sin, and redemption.

8. Observe the human touches in the Gospel narratives. Make note of those incidents that seem true to life. Note in what ways the biblical characters act and react as normal human beings.

Step 3: Study Background

In the study of a historical book like a Gospel, it is especially important to be aware of the geographical and historical background. Consult a Bible dictionary or encyclopedia for descriptions of people such as Pharisees and Sadducees, and for historical figures such as King Herod or Pontius Pilate. Locate on a map the events in the life of Jesus.

Step 4: Interpret

Although in the study of a longer book you may not record each question you ask yourself, still consider issues such as: Why is this event recorded? Why does Jesus do what he does? What is the meaning, significance, and implication of his statements, sermons, parables, stories? Why do people act and react as they do? Why is so much space given to some events and so little to others? What is the purpose of the author in recording these events? Why did the writer not record material that other Gospels included? As you chart the chapters and study individual paragraphs, write down some of your key *questions for understanding.*

When interpreting narrative passages, re-create in your own mind the historical situation. Imagine how you would have felt, acted, and reacted if you had witnessed the scene recorded. For example, try to re-create the thoughts and emotions of the disciples at the Transfiguration scene, at the Last Supper, and at his crucifixion.

Apply the same steps for interpreting narrative portions as you did with other passages: pray, meditate, define words, study characteristics of people, compare translations, look up cross-references, consult other helps. As always, summarize your findings.

Step 5: Summarize

Consider how to summarize what you have been studying. In Step 1, you charted the key information for the book. As you study each chapter more thoroughly, enlarge this chart to include many insights you have gained through your study. After a thorough study of a book, you might work out several charts, showing different aspects of the book.

As you summarize a book, note the way the writer has organized the material. It is helpful if you indicate this organization on your chart.

a) **Biographical:** in terms of the lives of people.
b) **Historical:** in terms of the succession of events.
c) **Chronological:** in terms of when events happened.
d) **Geographical:** in terms of the places where events happened.
e) **Logical or ideological:** in terms of the ideas themselves.

Step 6: Study Individual Passages

Study some of the more important passages, such as the special events in the life of Jesus, his sermons, or parables.

If it is a discourse passage such as one of Jesus' sermons, you will find it helpful to diagram it as is suggested in Chapter 8, making observations and asking yourself questions as you have done in your previous studies.

If it is a narrative, follow the suggestions in Chapter 5, Studying a Narrative. Use the words *where, when, who, what, why*, and *how* as your guides for observing details.

Step 7: Apply, Actualize

Application and actualization of biblical teachings are as important in studying the Gospels as they are in studying the epistles. Personalize the narratives as well as the exhortations and admonitions in the Gospels. Here are some ways:

When personalizing discourse material, ask questions like:

1. What are some truths to believe?

2. What are some promises to claim?

3. What are some attitudes and actions to follow?

4. What are some relationships to consider?

When personalizing narratives, follow these suggestions:

1. Read the story imaginatively, making the story your own.

2. Identify with one of the characters, one that seems to best reflect your feelings and concerns right now.

3. Determine where you are in terms of the experiences of this character. For instance, if you were to identify yourself with blind Bartimaeus (Mark 10:46-52), decide where you are right now:

a) sitting blindly by the side of a road
b) crying out to Jesus
c) hearing Jesus invite you to come to him
d) asking for a specific thing from him
e) experiencing his power
f) rejoicing in your new life

4. Identify the good news in the story for yourself.

13 Personalizing Biblical Teachings

To observe and interpret the facts are only the first two steps in discovery Bible study. There is little gained unless you apply the truths to your own life in a practical way. This chapter considers three aspects of personal appropriation of biblical teachings: *evaluation*, *application*, and *actualization*.

Evaluation—What Is the Value of Biblical Teachings?

In studying Scripture, you need to appraise the value of usefulness of a biblical teaching before you can apply it. This does not mean that you set yourself up as a critical judge, but with an honest heart continually appraise the general validity of a Bible passage in relation to present-day living. "Does the Bible have value for us today? Does it meet the needs of today's people? How valid is the message of a particular passage? To whom can these truths be applied?"

Suggestions for Evaluating:

The following questions may help you in evaluating a portion of Scripture.

1. What was the purpose of the writer? Is the purpose accomplished? Evaluate the worth of a passage with the writer's purpose in mind.

2. For whom was the Bible passage written? Strive to understand the setting, time, ethics of the day, the people to whom the book was written, and their experiences, customs, and needs.

3. What are general truths and what are local truths? Some passages of Scripture were written for a certain period of history and therefore are local in application. Bible students must distinguish between local truths applicable for specific time periods in history, and general truths that can be applied to any age. Although James wrote his epistle for a definite group of people, the statements he makes are equally applicable today. The Old Testament has some statements that cannot be applied to today, but behind every local truth there is usually a universal truth that can be applied in all ages.

4. What is the relation of the truths found in a particular passage to the whole message of the Bible? No single portion of Scripture should be evaluated apart from the whole message of the Bible. Consider biblical writings in their own context and in relation to the whole Bible message.

5. How valid is the translation? To judge the validity of a passage, it is best to read it in its original language. But if you cannot read Greek or Hebrew, compare translations to gain as clear a picture as possible of what the writer said.

6. How objective are you? Personal prejudices and pet whims should not govern your evaluation.

Application—What Do the Biblical Teachings Mean to Me?

In 2 Timothy 3:16-17, Paul states the general purpose of Bible study: "All Scripture is inspired by God and is useful for teaching the truth, rebuking error, correcting faults, and giving instruction for right living, so that the person who serves God may be fully qualified and equipped to do every kind of good deed" (TEV). The Bible study skills discussed here are only a means to an end: that God may accomplish good work in your life through the Word. Apply what you have learned, otherwise the study has not accomplished its primary purpose.

Ways to Apply Biblical Teachings

As you consider how to apply biblical teachings, there are several key questions you might ask yourself:

1. What am I to believe? One of the outcomes of Bible study is related to the doctrines and teachings that build faith. As you study a passage, ask yourself: "What is in this passage that I am to believe about God, Jesus Christ, the Holy Spirit, grace, mercy, sin, forgiveness, hope, eternal life, and so forth?"

2. What am I to do? Another outcome of Bible study concerns actions and attitudes. As you study a passage you might ask yourself some of these questions:

- **Actions:** How am I to reveal my faith through my actions? Are there actions that I need to change?
- **Attitudes:** What do I learn about positive and negative attitudes? What are the results of each kind? What do I learn about emotions? Is there help suggested for release from destructive emotions such as fear, worry, anxiety, hate, resentment, and jealousy?
- **Sin:** What sins are pointed out in my life? Are there some I need to confess to God? To my fellow members? That I need to forsake?

3. What do I learn about relationships? In the Bible, relationships are important. The Bible is a record of God's relationship with humankind and their response to this relationship. Christians may all believe that the Bible is the Word of God and yet vary a great deal in what they consider its truths.

Christianity is not so much "believing in the right things" as being involved in the "right relationships." One of the definitions of the term *righteous* is "right relationships." Your life as a Christian is based on your relationship with Jesus Christ, a relationship God made possible through the redemptive work of Christ. Christianity also is concerned about right relationships among human beings and with God's created world.

As you study a passage, consider what it has to say about relationships. Ask yourself the question: What does this passage say to me . . .

- about my relationship with God through Jesus Christ?
- about my relationship with others in my family? In my community? In my congregation? In the world?
- about my relationship with God's created world?
- about my relationship with myself?

4. What is the good news for me? This fourth question is probably the most personal of all. When studying a Bible passage, ask yourself, "Is there good news for me in this passage?" The Bible is the book of good news—the good news of God's reconciliation with God's children through Jesus Christ.

In study, expand your focus beyond the "bad news"—the bad news that all are sinners, failures, imperfect persons, never able to measure up to the demands of the Law. The good news of Christ is that Christians can approach Bible study without striving and struggling to meet the requirements of the Law. The good news is that Christ has done it all for each and every person.

Actualization—How Do I Personally Actualize Biblical Teachings?

To actualize means to bring into action those insights gained through your study. It is possible to intellectually apply biblical teachings but never really actualize them—make them a reality in your own life. To move from the intellectual assent to concrete reality is the challenge that all Bible students face. Here are some suggestions:

Meditate on the Teachings

To *meditate* is to contemplate and ponder some passages in a quiet, unhurried manner. In this day of hurry, fury, and worry, few spend much time in prayerful meditation. It is easy to do a little bit of reading and a little bit of praying, convinced that there is no time for more. Sit still long enough to give God time to speak to you. Practice meditation. Here are some things you might do:

- Relax your mind and body. Think of God's Spirit as releasing all your tensions.
- Read a passage slowly and prayerfully. Try reading it aloud.
- Consider what the passage has to say to you personally, using some of the questions suggested in "Ways to Apply Biblical Teachings" on pages 85-86.
- Imagine the Lord speaking to you through the passage.
- Reflect on the passage as a guide for prayer in terms of confession, petition, intercession, thanksgiving, and praise.

Express Your Faith in Concrete Ways

There are many ways to express your faith:

- Proclaim the good news of Jesus Christ in your home, community, and world.
- Reflect the sincerity of your faith in your willingness to share time, money, and energy in helping the needy, the lonely, the sick, and the aged.
- Be willing to become involved in church and community action groups in the struggle against poverty, racism, and prejudice.
- Speak of your faith creatively in poems, hymns, letters, and articles.
- Express concepts that are important to you through illustrations, drawings, banners, pictures, and construction projects.

Share Convictions and Concerns with Others

If in your Bible study you become concerned about some problem, need, or issue, it is helpful to share this with others. This is one of the values of studying in a small group. You will find that other group members may share the same concern. Together you can consider possibilities and encourage each other in potential actions.

Make a Commitment

Just sharing or discussing an issue or problem is not enough. There is need to make definite decisions and commitments. Unless you verbalize your feelings and decisions, you may have difficulty taking action. After discussing it with others, writing or speaking your commitment may give you greater strength and courage to carry out your plans.

Pray with One Another

Prayer is a very important aspect of actualizing biblical teaching. All need the help, power, guidance, and strength of the Lord. Pray individually about your decisions and seek the prayers of others as well. Praying with others provides additional strength for carrying out the commitments you make.

14

Discovering with Others

When Christians come together on Sunday morning for worship, it can be mainly an individual experience. Believers also need to meet in small groups to help each other grow in Christian faith. The church is a fellowship of believers. The term *fellowship* implies a close relationship with others, a sense of belonging, a caring for one another, a bearing of each other's burdens. A small-group Bible study is one of the places in which these things can happen.

Your Role in a Group

As a member of a Bible study group, there are at least four roles you may assume:

As a receiver. You may or may not have done much studying before the meeting, but your primary purpose for attending the meeting is to receive. You hope to receive something from the leader and possibly from other members in the group. This has been the traditional role for many people involved in Bible studies. Receivers measure the success of the Bible study by what they received, whether disappointing or inspired, depending on the effectiveness of the leader.

As a giver. This is the role assumed by leaders of Bible classes who invest much time in study before the meeting and come prepared to give. *Givers* see the other group members as receivers.

As receiver-giver. Group members assuming this role study before the meeting and come prepared to both give and receive from the others. If you are a *receiver-giver*, you hope to involve the group members in discussion so that all can give and receive from one another.

As an enabler. If you view yourself as an *enabler*, your concern will include the group members and what is happening to them. To *enable* means to call forth, to allow to emerge, to help someone else realize her or his potentials. To be an enabler means to call forth the best in each member of the group, enabling each person to share ideas, hopes, and concerns. An enabler is one who blesses and helps others to be a blessing.

Why Become Enablers?

To have the most positive results, a Bible study should have two dimensions: *vertical* (the Bible discoverer's relationship with God), and *horizontal* (the Bible discoverer's relationship with others). The most immediate way to enhance the horizontal dimension of Bible study is to strengthen relationships with other study group members.

Countless people have attended Bible studies, feeling lonely and discouraged, and have gone home feeling just as lonely and discouraged. The message contained hope for them, but they were unable to make the message their own. They needed to express their feelings, doubts, fears, and questions. They needed help in personalizing God's message of hope, love, grace, and mercy. Even though there are opportunities for discussion, unless group members feel welcomed and accepted by others in the group, they will not share their true feelings.

Group members become enablers when they are willing to share with others their thoughts, fears, and doubts. As enablers, group members seek to establish a climate of trust, acceptance, and understanding in which all can be free to share hopes and dreams, doubts and fears. The affirmation of others will help group members think new thoughts about themselves and their identity as children of God.

How to Become Enablers

Be concerned about each other's personal growth. The very way you treat each other in your group will create an enabling climate in which all can grow.

- Encourage each other to share feelings as well as ideas.
- Listen carefully to one another's contributions and add to them.
- Be careful not to dominate a discussion.
- Be open and honest in sharing doubts, fears, frustrations, as well as hopes and dreams.
- Respect one another's ideas.
- Allow one another the right to her or his opinion without judgment.
- Encourage those who are hesitant about sharing.
- Identify with the problems of others.

Express your concern for each other in concrete ways.

- Study for your group meeting, especially if you have accepted the responsibility for some special assignment.
- Be faithful in attendance. If you cannot attend, let the group know.
- Affirm, encourage, and support each other in what is said and done.
- Try to help one another identify each other's gifts.
- Care for those who express troubled feelings.
- Be sensitive to the feelings of others.
- Pray for and with one another.

Author's Closing Message

As I come to the end of the book, I would like to share with you my prayer that through these suggestions you have discovered . . .

- the joys of studying the Bible in a systematic way.
- the value of studying and sharing together with others.
- the power of the Holy Spirit to guide you in your study.
- the reality of the love and grace of Jesus Christ.
- the potentials and gifts the Lord has given you and ways you can use them in ministry.
- new insights in how to develop more satisfying relationships with others.
- greater concern for the needs of others.
- greater freedom, peace, and joy in your personal life as you learn to live in the grace and forgiveness of Jesus Christ.